SUPER
SEARCHERS
In
the NEWS

The Online Secrets of
JOURNALISTS AND NEWS RESEARCHERS

SUPER
SEARCHERS
In the NEWS

The Online Secrets of
JOURNALISTS AND NEWS RESEARCHERS

Paula J. Hane
Edited by Reva Basch

CyberAge Books

Information Today, Inc.
Medford, New Jersey

First Printing, 2000

Super Searchers In the News:
The Online Secrets of Journalists and News Researchers

Copyright © 2000 by Paula J. Hane

Super Searchers, Volume V
A series edited by Reva Basch

Library of Congress Cataloging-in-Publication Data

Hane, Paula J., 1949-
    Super searchers in the news : the online secrets of journalists & news researchers /
      Paula J. Hane ; edited by Reva Basch.
        p. cm. – (Super searchers ; v. 5)
    "CyberAge Books" –T.p.
    Includes bibliographical references and index.
    ISBN 0-910965-45-5
    1. Electronic news gathering. 2. Internet searching. 3. Journalists—United
States—Interviews. I. Basch, Reva. II. Title. III. Series.

PN4784.E53 H36 2000
025.06'0704—dc21

00-058122

Printed and bound in the United States of America

Publisher: Thomas H. Hogan, Sr.
Editor-in-Chief: John B. Bryans
Managing Editor: Janet M. Spavlik
Copy Editor: Dorothy Pike
Production Manager: M. Heide Dengler
Cover Designer: Jacqueline Walter
Book Designer: Jeremy M. Pellegrin
Indexer: Sharon Hughes

Dedication

To my parents Le and Jean for always believing in me
and
To Carl, Chris, and Phil for all the support and love

About The Super Searchers Web Page

At the Information Today Web site, you will find *The Super Searchers Web Page*, featuring links to sites mentioned in this book. We will periodically update the page, removing dead links and adding additional sites that may be useful to readers.

The Super Searchers Web Page is available as a bonus to readers of *Super Searchers in the News* and other books in the Super Searchers series. To access the page, an Internet connection and Web browser are required. Go to:

www.infotoday.com/supersearchers

Table of Contents

Foreword

I'm in Love with a Voice at Extension 2350

(pathetic play on the words of Judy Holliday's song in the 1960 musical *Bells Are Ringing*)

Research is reporting.

It's Friday night, and fingers fly. We are in the last, agitated hours of preparing for our Saturday morning broadcast, and I reach for the office phone to ring up the folks at X-2350 as frequently as—no, *more* frequently than I quaff another swig of coffee.

"Reference!" they answer, with reassuring zing. I have learned to read that vim as a friendly challenge: "Whaddya got?" Earlier in the day, the voice tends to be that of Kee Malesky. Earlier in the week, before weekend crews come in, it is often Caleb Gessesee. Later on Fridays, Alphonse Vinh is commonly left alone to finesse our inquiries. Sometimes, it is Barbara van Woerkem. (I like to think it is the inconvenience of the time shift, not the companionship, that's responsible for the changing cast.)

Since the start of our workweek, the folks at X-2350 have been passing along research, answering inquiries, and guiding our pronunciation. But on Friday nights, the inquiries become pointed and urgent.

We have decided to open our show with quick com-memoration of the fact that "On this date in 1974, Henry Aaron of the Atlanta Braves took one swing, and moved one step ahead of the great Babe Ruth in the record books: ROLL TAPE: 'Here's the pitch by Downing ...'"

The tape is a recording of the radio call made in 1974. Announcer Milo Hamilton furnishes the fact that the homer stroke was Henry's Aaron's 715th. But, a generation later, another question is suggested: How many did Hank Aaron end his career with? What was the new record he began to set with that swing? I seem to recall that this number was 755. But most of the mistakes in this world are committed by people who are confident that they know something. I punch up X-2350 and humble myself to ask. Within three minutes, Alphonse has gone to the online Major League player registry and the Baseball Encyclopedia to confirm that, on this one narrow point, my memory is accurate: Hank Aaron hit 755 home runs.

So, after the end of the tape clip ("... there's a new home run champion of all-time, and it's Henry Aaron!"), we are able to add: "Henry Aaron ended his career with 755 home runs. Ken Griffey Jr., keep that number in mind!"

We want to open the next hour by noting that, in that week, Vietnam began to construct its first superhighway. X-2350 has sent down clips from *The New York Times* and wire services noting that the road traces a route along the old Ho Chi Minh Trail. I write that "During the war in Vietnam, the Trail was a knotted network of jungle roads over which the North Vietnamese moved troops and ammunition into the South. The U.S. tried to destroy the Trail with billions of bombs ...."

Now, "billions of bombs" is a nice, euphonious phrase. But is it precisely true? Alphonse Vinh (who, it is irresistible to add, is part of the vast migration of talented Vietnamese who came to settle in the United States because of that conflict) confirms that the United States dropped 1.3 billion tons. But, of course, the heaviest bombs sometimes weighed a ton or more. And how many were actually dropped onto the old Ho Chi Minh Trail? So, according to Alphonse's instructions, I change the phrase to "The U.S. tried to destroy the trail with an abundance of bombs ...," which is euphonious, has rhythm, balance, and the added advantage of being accurate.

Another small item in the show (we call them Infos, for Information Breaks) notes that the Smithsonian had decided against stuffing the body of Hsing-Hsing, the panda who had been euthanized the previous autumn after suffering kidney failure. The folks at X-2350 have sent along the accounts from *The Washington Post*, which seem both compelling and complete. But *The Washington Post* doesn't have to pronounce the name of the late panda. Even if your facts are in order, a mispronunciation promotes an impression of inaccuracy; at the least, it is also a kind of misinformation. The newsroom (X-2100) is often our first call for the pronunciation of the name of a new Russian president, or winner of the first round of the Davis Cup. But where does a man go when he needs to know how to pronounce the name of a deceased panda? Once more, I reach out for X-2350. It is Barbara von Woerkem.

"Say," I ask, "how do you pronounce the name of the panda who died last fall? It's spelled like H-sing-H-sing?"

"I think it's pronounced," she says, "Shing-Shing. But I'll have to check and call you back." She consults the Reference Library's own online listing of pronunciations (I could have done this, I suppose; I just didn't think to. That's what happens when you have a relationship of dependency) and rings me back within a minute.

"Shing-Shing for shure," Barbara sibilantly announces.

"Shank you!" I tell her.

Not to be outdone, she adds, "Always at your shervice!" I wince a little upon realizing, once more, that the wittiest people on our staff are not the ones who will be on-the-air in a few hours.

Research is reporting. As the City News Bureau in Chicago still instructs its novitiates, "If your mother says she loves you, check it out." Even if you absolutely know the panda's name was pronounced Shing-Shing—check it out.

I don't know exactly where those at X-2350 go to become such accomplished know-it-alls. I can infer, from what they pass on to me, that they combine traditional reference sources (increasingly online), newspaper and magazine clips (also increasingly online), Web pages, and our own archived broadcasts (also—are you picking up on a trend here?—online) to ferret out and confirm information. And, while the folks at X-2350 are so reliably at our shervice, it's a real, two-way relationship. Kee Malesky is an information voyager who often regrets having to sail past interesting islands of knowledge, and notes their coordinates for us. Quite a few story and interview ideas originate with her and the other folks at X-2350.

But the stories they steer us away from can be just as valuable. I became intrigued with the public reaction to the retrieval of Elian Gonzalez from the home of his Miami relatives. When politicians and citizens would remark, "I've never seen anything like that before," I irresistibly remembered that I had. As a reporter, I've seen two raids by La Migra—the Immigration and Naturalization Service—in homes and factories. In both, the officers arrived armed and armor-clad, to discourage disagreement.

But when I asked Kee to try to determine the number of such raids that occur each year, she went online and on the phone with agencies and archives. She discovered that the INS had largely gone out of the business of pre-dawn raids. Publicity was so bad that they had not staged such actions for about eight years. The Gonzalez case was a phenomenon, not federal business as usual. Kee saved us—hell, saved me—from making a public overstatement that would have been inaccurate and misleading—not good reporting.

The lines between media are beginning to blur. Video and audio are online; online information increasingly moves, bleeps, and does the shimmy-shake. But in a sense, this new admixture that's beginning to emerge simply confirms that the ultimate target of all research and reporting is knowledge. And when the knowledge is all spread out before us, as beckoning and overwhelming as the northern sky, you need skilled professionals with a sure sense of guidance to steer you toward the right light. That's when we ring X-2350. If I ever had to have heart surgery, I suppose I'd want Dr. Michael DeBakey to do the job. But assuming he was unavailable, I'd punch up X-2350 and ask Kee or Alphonse, "Do you think you can brush up on a little something for me over the next few days?"

Scott Simon
Host, *Weekend Edition Saturday*
National Public Radio
Washington, DC

All examples quoted herein are from the Weekend Edition Saturday broadcast of April 8, 2000.

Acknowledgments

I am extremely grateful to the ten Super Searchers profiled in this book. Not one even hesitated when I approached them with the request for their time and for their expertise. They were all most gracious and cooperative, even when I returned with numerous questions and points of clarification as I edited the interviews, or when I pestered them for photos. I enjoyed all of our conversations and learned a great deal from each of them. My hat is off to this superb group. You are a credit to your profession.

In particular, Nora Paul and Margot Williams were of great assistance in the planning stages. I used them as my sounding boards for people and questions, and I appreciate their valuable input. After two book projects together, I now count them as dear colleagues and friends.

John Bryans, editor-in-chief, has been a valued colleague, friend, and, as he describes it, co-conspirator, for many years. Despite my initial hesitance, he urged me to dig into this project and has been a continuing supporter and cheerleader. I thank him for his confidence in my work and for offering me the opportunity to be part of the Super Searcher gang.

My editor, Reva Basch, and I have a long history of collaboration, though this time our roles were reversed. I was delighted to find that she is just as meticulous an editor as she is a writer. Her guidance throughout the process has been most appreciated.

I am also grateful to Dorothy Pike, who transcribed the taped interviews quickly and accurately—not a small task! She also did a final copy edit and her keen eyes caught things that slipped past ours. I've known Dorothy since her days as managing editor of *Information Today*, so I was pleased to have the chance to work with her again. Janet Spavlik, managing editor of CyberAge Books, has cheerfully kept us all on task and managed to bring this book to print.

Finally, I'd like to thank my family and friends for their extra patience and support during this project.

Paula J. Hane
Plano, Texas
August 2000

Introduction

I love the word "web." Building on the visual image of a spider's handiwork, it seems to embody so much in its three short letters—an intricate network interconnecting and forming a complex structure. In my mind, it's the perfect choice for our networked online infrastructure, the World Wide Web, which so handily connects people and information. A web is also a useful way to envision the complex interconnections of our current news and information environments. It also describes how I build a news story. I am both a consumer and a producer of news and information.

I love to do online research and I love the news. I worked first as a reference librarian in a college, teaching research methods. I've been an online searcher since the early '80s, and an early adopter and promoter of PC technology, email, and the Web. I was editing *Database* (now *EContent)* magazine when we made the transition from a print-based production mode to electronic publishing and electronic communications with authors. Margot Williams and Nora Paul, both interviewed in this book, wrote articles for me for *Database* about searching online information resources. Reva Basch, editor of the *Super Searchers* series and a Super Searcher herself, wrote one of her first published articles for me back in 1989. She's been a valued colleague and friend ever since, as we keep in touch from our virtual workplaces, building and maintaining our web of contacts.

Back then, of course, the resources we searched were databases on the traditional online services, and most of them were just bibliographic—full-text databases came later. Increasingly, I came to benefit from my connections on the Net and the additional reach and access. I used the Net to follow trends and issues that would impact the search environment and to monitor the pulse of what researchers were discussing and needed to know. The Net became a valued news resource for me, personally and professionally.

Over the last several years, I have been researching and writing news and analyses about companies, products, and trends in the online information industry and the new information environment of the Internet. I write weekly NewsBreaks for the Information Today Web site [93, see Appendix], and I monitor many issues and technologies for news coverage within the newspaper. I rely on a combination of the Web and traditional online resources for my information needs, as I suspect most professional researchers now do.

Why?

Last year, I worked for many months on a book project with Margot Williams and Nora Paul, who were committed to sharing their knowledge of subject-specific research guides on the Web. Editing their book, *Great Scouts!* [231], allowed me to work closely with two of the best news researchers in the business, and to gain some insights into their research methods and some of the changes occurring in newsrooms. Then, when I was asked to do this news volume for the Super Searchers series, I was intrigued by the opportunity to interview these two experts as well as others doing news research. The chance to delve into the secrets of the best news researchers was just too good to pass up.

Who?

Starting with these two leaders in the world of news research, I aimed to include a representative sampling of kinds of researchers: librarians, reporters who do research, research editors to news anchors, independent journalists, and journalism educators and leaders. I selected a broad variety of people in terms of education, experience, and focus. Half of those I included have library science degrees; about a third have journalism training. Their subject backgrounds are diverse, ranging from political science to music, history, dance, and liberal arts. Their knowledge and interests are broad-ranging.

C.B. Hayden of ABC News, with music history and business research among his credentials, said, "I think a varied background is one of the best preparations for news research." He stressed that "strong problem-solving skills and thought processes" are an essential element, since he and his staff are called upon to handle "just about anything" on a daily basis.

Mary Ellen Bates, in her book about business research, *Super Searchers Do Business,* said, "The Super Searchers I interviewed are people who like finding answers, who like pushing their limits, and who enjoy the thrill of the hunt as they discover new ways to find information." I think this basic approach is what characterizes all Super Searchers—loving that intellectual challenge. News researchers, in particular, have no time to waste or to be bored. After all, as Margot Williams of *The Washington Post* noted, news reporting is working on what Philip Graham called a "first rough draft of a history." This is important stuff.

All of those I interviewed have an insatiable curiosity and determination to track down the facts. All of them stressed that they have to be prepared, and then to think fast and get it right. They have to be willing to put their work on the line and stand responsibly behind it. Hayden said, "It's gratifying and scary at the same time to pick up a phone, give somebody a very quick answer, and literally thirty seconds later hear it come out of Peter Jennings' mouth."

Where?

I also wanted to include news researchers from all kinds of media—newspaper, newsmagazine, broadcast (including major networks and radio), books, and the Web. I wanted to explore the differences and similarities in what they did, why and how they did it, and how much influence their work settings and the size of their organization played.

I found that there's increasingly a cross-media approach, even a convergence of media. The researchers working for newspapers are also serving the needs of the paper's Web reporting and Web presence. Sometimes they are called to assist radio and TV affiliates. Researchers at the networks are involved in TV broadcast, Web sites, Webcasting, and sometimes beyond. Several of the independent journalist researchers are ubiquitous—writing books; writing articles for newspapers, newsletters, and magazines; reporting and producing radio and TV programming; hosting Web sites; and doing Webcasts. These are busy and hardworking folks, but they are also having fun.

Most of these researchers are also educators. Some are teaching news research in library schools and journalism programs. These researchers are training the present and future generations of research journalists. Nora Paul is a faculty member at the prestigious Poynter Institute for Media Studies, which holds seminars on news research and news library management, computer-assisted reporting, and leadership in new media newsrooms. Countless journalists and researchers around the country have benefited from her instruction and guidance over the years. She is also much in demand as a speaker at journalism conferences and has given Internet training sessions around the world. She has recently been appointed Director of the Institute for New Media Studies at the University of Minnesota School of Journalism and Mass Communications.

The researchers within news organizations are actively involved in training sessions, workshops, and one-on-one training with other researchers and journalists. Many are active as speakers, trainers, and authors, sharing generously of their knowledge and expertise—as they also have done by agreeing to be included in this book. Most of these folks are active participants and leaders in key news media professional organizations such as the News Division of the Special Libraries Association, Investigative Reporters and Editors, the Freedom Forum, and the National Institute for Computer Assisted Reporting.

Annabel Colley heads up the Association of UK Media Librarians and keeps in close touch with professional colleagues in the United States. Duff Wilson of the *Seattle Times* started his Reporter's Desktop Web site for himself, then generously shared it with his journalism colleagues, who in return provide valued feedback and suggestions. T.K. Maloy is a professor of new media and writes *The Internet Newsroom*, a newsletter that helps journalists and researchers by sifting through and recommending new sites, services, and technologies and by providing tips and guidance. Mike Wendland, who writes and speaks widely about the Internet, has been appointed a Fellow at the Poynter Institute. In 1996 and 1998, as the recipient of the Special Libraries Association/Freedom Forum fellowship, Margot Williams traveled to Hong Kong and Manila to train journalists in the use of the Internet.

How and When?

To start, I spent several months immersing myself in the news research and computer-assisted reporting networks. I signed onto discussion lists to see what sorts of issues were being discussed, gradually extending my reach across the web of news media connections. Since all of my recent news research was done on my own and focused on the information industry, I searched for and read articles and books about what was happening in newsrooms. I probed and queried colleagues for ideas on people, issues, and trends.

Then, armed with my tape recorder and a head full of ideas and potential questions, I conducted telephone interviews with my hand-picked group. I chose not to do an email exchange of questions and answers, even with my interviewee from the BBC in the U. K. The substance and interplay of dialogue with these experts often determined the course of questioning, and I felt the spontaneous nature of our discussion to be a valuable asset.

What?

Super Searchers in the News consists of interviews with ten news researchers and journalists who are on the front line daily. Nine are from the U. S. and one is from the prestigious investigative reporting unit of the BBC in the U. K. They are expert searchers across a broad range of services and the Internet. In fact, they are stretched to almost unmanageable lengths in trying to keep up with the burgeoning choices for information access and make decisions about the best search venue for the needs at hand.

Searchers today have more information and better access to information than at any time in history, but we also face some interesting challenges in negotiating the information landscape. Searchers have to pick and choose their way amid a dizzying array of sources and access. It's not a simple choice, even if you know exactly what document you want. You might have to contend with where and how to get it—free or from a fee-based or subscription service—not to mention how to get it most easily, quickly, and in the most accurate form. These expert news researchers are the ones serving as scouts and guides to others in their organizations and in the news business.

I asked these news researchers what I wanted to know and understand about what is happening today in news research. I probed them about the changing nature of research given the impact of technology and the Internet, about the working relationships of researchers and reporters, about managing the variety of information resources, about data integrity, and about leveraging information. I solicited their best tips for choosing sources, evaluating resources, and tackling news projects. Okay—I did the basic "who, what, where, when, how, why" routine on them.

Trends and Themes

The last several years have seen dramatic changes in almost all aspects of our lives, personal and professional. We are more wired, tuned-in, and Web-connected than almost anyone could have imagined. In fact, we're quickly moving beyond wired to wireless connections. Like other sectors of our increasingly digital society, both news reporting and its underlying research support are undergoing tremendous change. As Nora Paul points out, "It used to be that the Internet was an interesting supplement. But increasingly the news is happening *on* the Web, the news is happening *about* the Web. If you're not able to get to the Web and use it well, it's like not being able to get to the crime scene and do your reporting."

The word "Internet" wasn't even mentioned in Reva Basch's 1993 volume, *Secrets of the Super Searchers* [238]. Nora Paul was one of the people included in that book, and her concern at the time had to do with newspapers making their databases available exclusively on CD-ROM, thereby reverting to single-source searching, disk swapping, loss of currency, and costly purchasing of disks. We've certainly come a long way in a short time.

Several years of concerted efforts to get newsrooms wired and to train staff to be computer- and Internet-literate have paid off. Many newsrooms have worked hard to improve information access, and we can now see the results of these efforts. One major benefit has been much improved access to newspapers, magazines, and broadcast material online. Several of the interviewees tell stories from the past about trying to find out what was published and available in other publications and media, and then trying to obtain copies.

Technological advances and the Net have not only changed the communication among researchers, reporters, and their sources, but it has expanded their reach in terms of the amount, depth, and breadth of access to sources, and has expanded their contact with, and distribution to, a global audience. Also, things are moving at a much faster pace. Many of the interviewees tell stories comparing how they can research in minutes or hours what used to take days and months.

Many newsrooms with technology-savvy researchers and reporters are moving to add end-user searching of commercial databases using Web interfaces. Services like Lexis-Nexis Universe have become popular because of their easy interfaces and flat-fee pricing. Many newsrooms already have, or are working to implement, newsroom or corporate intranets that offer a range of direct links to search services, proprietary databases such as public records data, and categorized recommendations of Web resources.

The intranet allows reporters to do much of their own researching, which in turn allows the librarians and specialized researchers to act as trainers, guides, problem solvers, and organizers of information and gives them more time to do the difficult and problematic searching. Some of the larger newsroom organizations have worked with commercial vendors to design custom interfaces for their intranet access to services.

The trend in newsrooms shows researchers moving physically out of the library space and working next to reporters and editors, often as an integral part of the editorial team. Researchers are increasingly being recognized for their contributions, with bylines and credits and—even better—inclusion in teams that have been recognized by prestigious journalism awards. Both Margot Williams and Liz Donovan are Pulitzer Prize winners for their roles in the reporting process. True partnerships are beginning to emerge.

Back in July 1997, Nora Paul spoke at a NetMedia conference seminar, Media Libraries and New Media. It now appears that newsroom relationships are evolving as she envisioned:

"This evolutionary change in role between the library and the newsroom will result in an information partnership where the librarian's skills as evaluator, tracker, and trainer of information will work with the reporter's role as interpreter, explainer, and compelling writer. Together, the news reporting will be more accurate, contain more perspective, bring in more voices, and provide different angles than possible in the past. ... This is not to say that the research role will be totally abdicated to the reporter. In a partnership, those with the greatest skills do the part of the job they can best get done. In a reporting crunch or for research requiring detailed and in-depth searching, the librarian/researcher's role will be an important contribution to the newsgathering."

These Super Searcher researchers are among those actively forging new roles and new titles for librarians and searchers. They are moving beyond serving as information keepers and intermediaries. To reflect their new roles within the news organizations, many of them now have new titles, such as research editor, research journalist, information editor, and reference editor.

Another trend that I see in news operations is that the successful newsroom knows how to share and communicate what it knows internally. In the business world it's called leveraging information assets, or knowledge management. In newsrooms, a number of things are contributing to this knowledge sharing, including the increasing proximity of researchers to reporters, integration of research into the reporting strategies and routines, training sessions and continuous research guidance, capture and archiving of important data, and intranets for easy access and communication. Technology has also enabled easier point-to-point communication and multiple communications among colleagues.

That is not to say that knowledge sharing comes easily for reporters, whose natural instincts are to protect their information sources and not share. In fact, several of the interviewees discussed the tensions inherent in the collaborative nature of the librarian/researcher versus the competitive mindset of the investigative reporter. Getting reporters to contribute content to the newsroom intranet appears to be an ongoing struggle.

Technological developments and the convergence of media

are also greatly changing the landscape of journalism and research. Most observers predict that our news in the 21st century will be a blend of text, audio, video, graphics, and data. Clear lines no longer exist between newspapers, Web sites, text, graphics, multimedia, TV, radio, PCs, or telephones. The Internet has touched every aspect of what these researchers and journalists do. Most have reporting or researching roles in a number of media. Mike Wendland embodies the new type of journalist, with his involvement encompassing books, newspapers, radio, TV, Web sites, and online Webcasts. He also talks about how the new technology allows him to extend his ability to research and communicate out in the field and on location.

When I asked these researchers to look to the future, some expressed concerns about "Internet time" influencing reporting accuracy and fact checking. Annabel Colley wondered whether in-depth analysis and investigation would suffer as we "continually strive to feed the appetite for live news in a 24-hour society." Most were very optimistic about the future roles for researchers within the news structure, and most saw continuing positive movement ahead for integrating information management and research into the entire news process. All of them were excited by technological improvements and looked forward to more exciting involvement in shaping the news of the future.

I wondered how to arrange the interviews in the book. Should I put them in the order that I actually did the interviews? Should I group them by similar topics, concerns, or themes? Should I just consider intuitively how the interviews would flow from one to another? I finally opted to group them *roughly* by media type, even though the interviewees certainly play multiple roles and are involved in multiple media. Once I decided to do this, the ten interviews fell into place rather well and do complement each other. Of course, reading straight through is not required. You can hop and skip through, however it suits you.

Nora Paul's influence in the world of news research will be clear, however, when you see how many of the people interviewed here refer to her ideas and recommendations and have put them into practice. Thus, I begin the book with Nora, the educator, and move on to another educator who is also a reporter, then to a reporter for a newspaper, followed by several researchers for magazines and newspapers. Ubiquitous Mike Wendland then follows and provides the transition to my broadcast media representatives.

For the sake of readability, we did not include the Internet addresses for all the sites and services mentioned in the interviews. We compiled all these resources into a single Referenced Sources section in the Appendix. The first mention of each resource in a chapter is noted with a number corresponding to the list. The sources include Internet sites, search engines, online databases, electronic discussion groups, mailing lists, electronic newsletters, journals, books, and software.

This compilation of resources serves as a record of what these ten Super Searchers use and recommend on a daily basis—the best of the best resources for researchers and journalists. This valuable list with links is available, along with links from the other books in the Super Searchers series, on *The Super Searchers Web Page* at the Information Today Web site (www.infotoday.com/supersearchers). We will periodically update the page, removing dead links and adding additional sites that may be useful to readers.

I am most grateful to this group of researchers for generously sharing their experiences and recommendations with me and our readers. The resources listed in the Appendix are a valuable contribution to their colleagues. But, what I most enjoyed about the chance to talk with these ten Super Searchers was hearing their stories, learning from their insights and advice, gaining from their tips and suggestions, and growing from their knowledge. I trust you will too.

Nora Paul
Search Instructor and
News Librarian Icon

Nora Paul is a faculty member of the Poynter Institute, a school for journalists in St. Petersburg, Florida. She is responsible for holding seminars in the areas of news research and news library management, computer-assisted reporting, and leadership in new media newsrooms. She is also a well-known speaker, author, and consultant. She was recently appointed Director, Institute for New Media Studies, at the University of Minnesota, School of Journalism and Mass Communications.

npaul@umn.edu
www.poynter.org
www.sjmc.umn.edu

Tell me about your news background and how you came to be at the Poynter Institute.

I had always wanted to get into media libraries. After library school, I moved to Houston, Texas, and tried to get a job at the *Houston Chronicle*, but wasn't able to, so I ended up at the public library. Soon thereafter, I started an information brokerage service with another colleague at the public library. But when I heard about a job opening at *The Miami Herald*, I applied for it and got the position. That was in 1979. I spent twelve years at *The Miami Herald* as the research library director, and then became the editor for information services. In 1991, I came over to the Poynter Institute. At Poynter, I got to start promoting the whole area of news research and news library management.

13

I imagine that the research you did at *The Miami Herald* used mostly the traditional online services.

Yes, for the most part, we used the big commercial database services, although we were blessed in Florida to have earlier online access to public records. So, by about the mid-1980s, we started gathering information about how we could access public records online. In 1989, I prepared a guide to computer-accessible public records in Florida State agencies and in Dade and Broward County agencies. The other thing I became fascinated with in the late 1980s was online bulletin board services and the ability of these subject-focused bulletin boards to provide interesting angles and leads for reporters.

I suspect that, at that time, research was pretty much focused in the library, and the reporters would come to you with requests. Is that how it worked?

Yes. It was definitely the era of the gatekeeper. In many ways, we were the economic gatekeepers, because the commercial services were very expensive, and there was the feeling that having reporters accessing these databases and muddling around and wasting money was a highly inefficient and expensive enterprise. So, definitely, researcher-as-gatekeeper was the mode in the 1980s.

Tell me a little about the kinds of courses and programs at Poynter.

My initial interest was promoting a constituency that Poynter did not really have when I came here—the news librarian. The previous library director at Poynter had started a news library management course and had set the foundation; I carried on with that. That seminar was really for the people who were running the news research center. It focused on how to get them to make their position more powerful and market it better.

Then we moved on to some programs that promoted the idea of news research in general, particularly as Internet resources grew. Clearly the move was under way from researcher/gate-keeper to information end user. So we started programs to train end users in how to use these resources well. We've always structured those courses so that researchers and reporters would come at the same time. It's been a wonderful cross-pollination. The researchers get a chance to see how reporters and editors really think and approach the newsgathering for a story, and the reporters and editors definitely gain a new respect for the kinds of skills that researchers bring to their work.

I've seen some comments about news researchers becoming more like reporters, and reporters becoming more like news researchers. Is this good? Are you seeing teams like this working on projects in news organizations?

That's definitely the trend. As researchers get themselves out of the corner that the library was in and more into the news flow, their contribution to the initial newsgathering has been growing. An indication of this is the number of news stories that now credit a researcher as one of the people contributing to the story. It's a wonderful thing. That kind of team reporting is definitely the trend.

I also think that a good researcher is a good reporter and a good reporter is a good researcher. The main difference between the two is that reporters tend to concentrate on primary sources—they talk to people, they really analyze documents—whereas researchers tend to specialize in secondary sources—the kind of information that's filtered and edited and usually published somewhere else.

How do you recommend that reporters and researchers become comfortable with Net research and sites? How do you help them get up to speed?

There is no shortcut, really. It just takes time. My main advice for researchers and reporters is to think very small about the Internet. If you feel that you have to know all of it in order to know any of it, you're doomed. The best approach is to analyze the kinds of research needs that you have on a routine basis. Look at the ways you satisfy those research needs and see if there are Internet-available alternatives that can either supplement the techniques that you use now or, as I see increasingly, *replace* the techniques that you use now. For example, if you routinely go to five different major publications because you like to see what people have covered in those publications, look at how you might access those publications in the Internet world. Or, if you routinely have to find certain kinds of documents or press releases, or you rely on information from particular companies or industries, analyze whether information that's available on the Internet could satisfy those needs. Be very focused; look at information tasks and then try to find the tool that will help you get the task done.

But information on the Net has grown dramatically. When you can find the same information in a number of places—let's say it's on the traditional online services with very powerful search tools, and it's also on the Net with very limited searching capabilities—this presents an interesting choice. Do I get it free and struggle with it? Or do I use a professional service and pay a lot?

Right. It depends on the person who's trying to get the task done. If you're an information professional, you have a tolerance and an expectation for more sophisticated search capabilities. But, like it or not, we are moving into an end-user environment. If you stand in front of a group of end users and say "Boolean logic," nineteen out of twenty will not know what you're referring to. Also, as people start making better information commodity choices, analyzing the available options becomes even more of a challenge. You can get *The Dallas Morning News*, for example, in seven different places online. Which one lets you get it most efficiently? Which one lets you get it with the most targeted search? Which one lets you get it the cheapest? You'll get different answers, depending on those three things. It goes back to "What do you value most?"

What can people do to help sort through those decisions? First of all, how do you discover that a source is available in seven different places, and then, how do you decide where to get it?

This is why, when information professionals worry about being shut out of a job because of end-user searching, I just have to laugh. If anything, the need for analyzing, selecting, categorizing, and making available information resources is going to grow and grow as the numbers of resources grow. There's a new job for the news researcher as evaluator and qualifier and analyzer of the different sources available, and as creator of pathfinders and other resources to help end users use the resources. It's going to be less hands-on "I'm going to type up the search request on the keyboard," and much more "If you need this kind of resource, here's what we've determined is the best place to get it." It's going to be a really important job. It's no different from what a collection development librarian has always had to do, but the range of sources to select from is so much broader than the ten key book-publishing catalogs or whatever they used to select books from in the past.

What advice do you give your reporters and end users about dealing with data integrity and authority of material found on the Internet? How do you help them evaluate sources and sites?

When you ask journalists what their main concerns are about using the Internet, number one is "There's too much information out there; I can't do a good search that lets me narrow it down." Number two is "How do I know I can trust what I find?" To me, one shame of most newsrooms is that they don't spend enough time training people on the use of this incredible, powerful information tool that they've got on their desktops now. The training that does go on is too centered on the mechanics rather than the critical thinking. The critical thinking skills involved in online resource evaluation and credibility checking are not much different from the critical thinking skills that journalists already use to judge the usability or reliability of other kinds of information that they encounter.

It seems odd to me that, when that same information is delivered through the Internet, all the old backgrounding, reality checking, and bullshit-detection skills fly away. People get so anxious. So, one of the courses that I teach, and consider to be a real keystone of the Internet seminar, is on credibility. We take a broad topic, do a search-engine search, and come up with a variety of hits. We start training them to make some quick value judgments: What can you tell from the Web address that would indicate whether this is likely to be reliable or not? Can you tell if this is a personal page, or if this is from a government source? How can you make a quick first evaluation of whether a site is even worth going out to? Then, once you pull up the page, what are the basic criteria for looking at the information on that page in order to judge whether it's something that you can rely on?

The criteria on evaluating information on the Web that the librarians from Widener University's Wolfgram Memorial Library [56, see Appendix] put together are great. The site is called Evaluating Web Resources, by Jan Alexander and Marcia Ann

Tate. I always send reporters there. They include wonderfully practical advice like "If you can't determine who has put this page together and there's *no* way to contact them to find out more about how they got this information, run the other way!" Why would you even spend time on it? After one of those credibility sessions, people are usually much more comfortable with their own abilities to make these basic choices.

Are reporters concerned about information that might disappear from sites or that might not be retrievable again? What about the problems of currency and permanence?

Yes, that is a huge issue. Archiving information on the Web is still such an open issue. Now, at least, we have some techniques for dealing with it. For example, if you use the search site Google [80] and locate a wonderful Web page, but get that "404 page not found" message when you try to navigate to it, you can click on "cache" in the corresponding entry in your results list, and Google will retrieve the page as it existed when Google last indexed it. So, Google can be used to track a disappearing URL. This is intriguing and brings up a whole additional set of questions. Pages sometimes disappear for very good reasons.

If it's not there any more, should you really rely on it?

Exactly. The Internet information space is, in many ways, no different from the information searching we did in the past with traditional sources. But in so many other ways, it's completely different. It's the differences that I find most intriguing, and also what makes being an information professional such an interesting job these days. I think it's really breathed a lot of new life into the profession.

You mentioned Google. What about your personal search preferences? Do you use broad search engines, metasearch engines, narrow sites, very specific subject-search sites? How do you recommend that people choose among all these possible tools?

We try to help people think very clearly about what they're trying to accomplish. One of the biggest shifts in approaching information on the Internet is how to move away from "clip-file heading" thinking. People who still approach research in terms of the "subject heading" are going to be swamped quickly. The most important thing is to think of the task first. For example, red tide just sprang up around the coast of Florida. In the past, you would have thought "red tide" and gone to the clip file under "red tide" and found the newspaper stories. That would have satisfied one kind of information task: "I need some background on red tide" or "What have we written about it?"

But in the world of the Internet, where you can get information from so many places and so many *types* of places, being clear about your task is important. So, at this point in your research, are you looking for a definition of red tide, in which case you might go to a good scientific or general encyclopedia? Or are you looking for other incidences of red tide around the country? Where would you go for that kind of information? What government agency would monitor that kind of event? I would look for a Web site for the appropriate agency—NOAA (National Oceanic and Atmospheric Administration) [192], or something like that. If you want to find experts to talk to about red tides, you would take a different path. The most important first step is to be very clear about what you're really trying to locate.

The next thing is to know the differences among the various kinds of Web locating tools—the value of a Yahoo!-type directory if all you need is a couple of good Web sites about red tides, versus a search tool that would let you locate obscure references to red tide. You also have to know how to narrow your resources to a specific topic or study area, and that means knowing the differences between a general search site versus one that specializes in environmental information.

One of the big challenges to me as a teacher helping others navigate the Web is making people more conscious about the resources that are available, and clearer about the task they're trying to perform. The goal is to marry those two and end up with a much more efficient and satisfying research experience.

Thinking about that red tide example, it strikes me that we have really expanded the possibilities for finding additional information. Think about a reporter going into a "red tide" story ten years ago, versus now. Now they have a universe of possibilities they could pull in.

Yes, and they can do it quickly. Internet-accessed information allows a whole new type of journalism. There's a great potential now for journalism to move beyond just event reporting, going to the usual suspects for comments, and staying provincial. The Internet is expanding what journalism itself can be.

The other thing that's intriguing about the Internet is how it has leveled the playing field for news organizations. In the past, the edge in reporting went to the person who had great clip files from a great newspaper, or had the big budget to be able to access those files, or lived close enough to be able to go and look at the records—the inside-the-Beltway advantage that Washington reporters had, for example. That's not really the case anymore. When the golfer Payne Stewart's plane went awry, reporters from all over the country were able to tap into the database of FAA plane information [188] and get the statistics on that particular aircraft. So reporters are able to be much more independent in news gathering and information gathering, and not have to rely on some other news source to tell them what's going on.

Do you use any email alert services?

Yes. I think the idea of alert services is intriguing and will increasingly be used by journalists who want to stay up-to-date on a beat or a topic area that they're interested in. I have experimented with some, such as Informant [92], particularly when I'm getting ready to speak to a group. I will set up a filter to tap into some particular topics so that I can show concrete examples of the kind of information that can be captured.

Alert services will capture and tell you about the very things that you won't be able to find in most of the major search sites. Search sites that rely on a spider or robot software to go out and index Web sites may only send the robot out once every six weeks. So the new information, the stuff that's fresh, the stuff that's really going to provide good news tips, will not necessarily be picked up by a search-site spider. But if you set up a current awareness filter, or go to the specific sites from which you would like to get information and sign up for their email newsletter update, you'll hear about those things much faster. There is a good list of alert services organized by beats at PowerReporting.com [145].

Another thing that's intriguing are the change-monitoring services, like Informant, where you put in the addresses of Web sites that you're interested in monitoring. Those are really important, especially for anybody following a particular beat.

I think that change monitoring is going to become a standard search tool, and that it's going to be increasingly important as the universe of information gets bigger.

Yes, especially as people's interests and needs become focused. There's always the concern on a big-circulation newspaper's Web site that the browsability you get in the print paper—the things you encounter that you didn't expect to—will be lost if you're able to personalize your interests too narrowly. I'm not quite as concerned as other people are about that; I think you do encounter the news you need to hear because there are so many ways to hear it.

What do you like best about Web research and what the Internet has to offer?

One of the things that has been most intriguing to me, after years of using the commercial article-archiving services, is the range of esoterica out there. Some of it is fascinating and can bring in some new and exciting facets to the research. You can get a newsletter that, in the past, only went to the thirty-eight people who subscribed to it. It's now available on a Web site. Some of these are extremely well-researched. The people who produce them are often the kind about whom other people say, "They should get a life." But this *is* their life. They know everything about growing orchids, or whatever, and they want to make it available to the world. So the tyranny of the mainstream media is busted. That's the good news. That's also the part that's quite scary, the part that gives you the credibility problem.

The other thing I find fascinating is that the Internet gets you to raw, primary sources; the old commercial services only got you to secondary sources. The Internet now offers the whole world of newsgroups, mailing lists, chat—all those places where you can find people and their opinions, unfiltered.

Which in turn has its good and bad sides. You can find a lot of bias.

Oh, absolutely. We teach that an agenda, in and of itself, is not a bad thing. Everybody's got an agenda. What's bad is when you don't know what the agenda is. The Internet's ability to get at a lot of "agendas" very quickly offers the potential of doing new kinds of journalism. We may see less black-and-white reporting and more shades of gray. That can only improve the journalism that we do.

I talk a lot about the dark side and the light side of the Internet, the yin and the yang. For everything that is a powerful good, there is a cautionary evil side. That's part of the consciousness-raising that we try to do with our Internet training. We don't let people use "What somebody says might be wrong; therefore, I don't need to use the Internet" as their excuse.

In the past, the Internet was an interesting supplement, but increasingly the news is happening *on* the Web, the news is happening *about* the Web. If you're not able to get to the Web and use it well, it's like you're not able to get to the crime scene and do your reporting. Also, because so many people are using the Web as an efficient and economical information distribution system, if you're not on the Web and able to get the information that you really need to do your job, you're going to be shut out. They're not sending out press releases by fax anymore. It's "Come to our Web site" or "Sign up for our email newsletter."

What do you find most frustrating about the Internet?

I don't ever find it *really* frustrating. Mostly, it's fascinating. I get frustrated when I get lulled into that "It must be here somewhere" mode, and I don't use my logic and go find it the way I used to find it. For example, I was trying to find the number of sunny days in Minneapolis, and I looked all over. Did I use my logic? No, I clicked all over—the National Weather Service [193], the Weather Channel [200], all kinds of places. Then I said, "I know I've seen this chart before," and then, "and I know *where* I've seen it"—the *World Almanac* [242]. I went over to the *World Almanac*, opened the printed book, and two seconds later I had the chart. So, I get caught in that kind of thinking. It's important to think logically about resources and remember that sometimes the best source is in print.

The other thing I do find frustrating is the incredibly bad design of so many information-rich sites, especially some of the news sites. A lot of the information sites are so unintuitive, even for someone with a high tolerance for poking around. So that's one of my campaigns: There should be a core of basic elements on any Web page, and basic design conventions. I once heard somebody say that we need to think about people who use the Internet, not as readers or as viewers, but as learners. How can we help these people *learn*? So many Web sites do anything *but* help facilitate learning.

Your earlier mention of "clip files" brings to mind the whole issue of preserving the results of one's research. So much is gathered now in electronic form. People are dumping massive amounts of information—organized or not—into their own computers. Do you get questions from research organizations about how to deal with their internal network of resources when it has become a digital resource? What advice do you give people about storing, sharing, and organizing what they have?

That brings in the sticky wicket of copyright, too, and I don't want to go there. The whole idea of "knowledge management" is going to be such a revolution. Everyone will have to be willing to contribute their knowledge to a knowledge management system, whether on an intranet or organized some other way, so that everyone else can access their information or thinking process. It has not occurred yet, but that shift is going to have to happen.

All those apparent technological challenges—"Is the hardware sufficient to store all this stuff? Is the software available to organize it and retrieve it?"—those are the simple problems to handle. It's not the hardware or the software. It's the "wetware," the people issues, that are going to be the real hurdles. How do you get people to shift their way of working and impose some kind of organizational structure on it? That's going be the major challenge.

Intranets are going to require an incredible amount of buy-in by individuals. That's going to be an interesting shift for news researchers—changing their focus from "I'm the one who takes it all in and organizes it" to "I'm the one who helps coordinate this group effort to make the collective intelligence available to everyone." It's team thinking, shared responsibility, and empowering people—those kinds of things—that are really the major shift.

Are you aware of any news organization that is doing cutting-edge work in this regard?

It's not so much cutting-edge as it is practical. The *San Antonio Express News* is doing a good job with intranets. Kathy Foley, the research editor, took to heart the idea that "this has to be everyone's invention." It's not supposed to be the library's invention; it's the newsroom's invention. I once heard Raymond Kurzweil say, "Let the people who need the invention do the inventing." Each of the news desks is responsible for its own intranet area. They have their staff directory, timesheets, and links to sources that are really good for that particular desk. Each desk can do whatever it wants in that Web area. Kathy's the consultant and guide and cheerleader, but she's not making the business desk Web site, and she's not making the sports desk Web site. They take it on as their own project. That's really the best approach.

We were talking earlier about search tips. Do you have any other search tips that you have found particularly useful?

One of the interesting things about Internet searching is that, even if you do an incredibly shoddy job of searching, the search engine saves you from yourself. Even without taking advantage of Boolean logic or the other advanced search techniques that might be available, you just throw in a couple of terms, and the first few hits are usually pretty right-on. It's hard to do Internet search training when, in fact, bumbling kinds of searches end up doing a fairly good job because of the sophisticated search-and-retrieval algorithms that are going on behind the scenes.

That must present a problem when a reporter says, "I already searched the Internet. I must have found everything."

Right. I draw a little circle of the Internet world, with all the continents and all the networks connected to each other. Then we start talking about search engines. When you slice the whole world of the Internet and indicate how much of it is covered by different search engines, people's jaws drop. It's a very small percentage. With Yahoo! [206], you're getting, what, maybe five percent of the Internet, if that much? The best of the search engine crawlers only covers about eighteen percent of the Internet now, and that percentage is getting smaller all the time. A couple of years ago, the largest of the search engines covered about thirty-four percent of the available Web pages; it has scaled back considerably because of the sheer growth of the Web.

Those graphic illustrations let people know that their simple search is not necessarily getting everything. And that goes back to the need for the discussion about "What are you *really* trying to do?" To anybody who says, "Oh, I haven't found everything," I say, "Well, good Lord, what would you do if you *did* find everything? Sit on a mountaintop and read for the next forty years?"

Perhaps that's what's driving the trend toward niche portals that gather information in very specific slices. Another searching trend is going after the "invisible Web," databases in a particular area that are behind a firewall or a password or whatever, that the search engines don't find. Increasingly, I think, those kinds of sites are going to be the answer to the "too much is out there" dilemma.

Right. But again, it's critical to be very focused on what you're trying to do. If you're looking for background on the insanity plea, you might use a general search engine. But if you know that what you really need is information from a legal-type source, then you'll use LawCrawler [105], which only indexes information from designated legal sites.

Specialized crawlers, or spiders, are going to be a big growth area. The original spiders went out willy-nilly and indexed Web pages throughout the Internet. What's happening now is that very specific, targeted Web sites are being spidered and, in effect, specialized search services are being created. In a lot of ways, it's like going back to the old *Social Sciences Index* or Dialog databases like the *Humanities Index* that only indexed the contents of 150 selected humanities-related journals, or whatever. Now we're getting the Web equivalent of the humanities spider that only goes out to the 150 designated Web sites that somebody's decided have good humanities content.

Isn't this access by specific subjects in fact the impetus behind the book that you and Margot Williams did?

Yes, our *Great Scouts!* book [231]. There are two different kinds of subject-specific search sites. One is the human-indexed site, where somebody has to look at a Web site, put it into a subject category, and organize references in a subject-categorized hierarchy. The book that Margot and I did is about those subject-specific human-indexed directories, where people have gone out and scouted around the Web, and have found Web sites that are good for particular topics and have put them into some kind of subject categorization.

The other kind of subject-specific search site is the "slice engines." They're more like the spiders that go out and scour the Web and then index the pages they find. We're upgrading the Web site at the Poynter Institute, and one of the new features that we're going to add is a variety of spider services. We bought Autonomy software [245], which allows us to create spiders. We have one, for example, that will spider the top-circulation newspapers and television stations from each state and about 150 international newspapers once a day, so that a journalist trying to cover a particular story can quickly see how other people have covered that story. We'll keep that data for about a week.

Then we're going to do ten beat spiders where we pick ten different topics and find, initially, twenty key Web sites—very credible, very usable, very rich-content Web sites—related to each beat. We'll spider those. So, when you do a search in the Poynter's medical spider [146], for example, you know you'll only get information from the Centers for Disease Control, the World Health Organization, the American Medical Association, places like that where you know you can trust the information. There will be a journalism spider; we're going to spider the journalism organization Web sites. *The Wall Street Journal* just did something like this with two thousand business-related Web sites [49]. I think this is what our next book has to be about!

I just heard of a Web clipping service called CyberClipping.com [37]. It monitors the 100 top online newspapers and thirty other top news resources, which could be useful for a reporter to see "How was this covered in other places?" I think services like that are going to become more prevalent.

Right. I don't know how anybody's going to make any money, but here in the Wild West of information, I guess anything is possible!

Yes, things are changing so quickly—it's sort of a dizzying pace sometimes. How do you think research and reporting could change over the next few years and how do you expect it to impact what researchers are doing?

I think the idea of the researcher as a coach and a mentor to reporters is going to grow. It also means researchers are going to be sitting out on the floor with the reporters to be part of the news flow. So there's going to be some walls tumbling down, and I think that's a very good thing. I think also the whole idea of researchers getting to know the kinds of information tasks that reporters have is going to have to be much more of a responsibility. Researchers will need to do a lot of interviewing of their clientele, their colleagues, "What do you do, how do you do it, why are you doing that, what do you need to find?" Researchers are going to have to focus on the specific information tasks and needs of their newsrooms.

One of the things that I find frustrating is the amount of do-over work that researchers are doing. Somebody's put together a wonderful resource list but then somebody else does, too, when they could feed on each other's work a little more efficiently. I think this is going to be important. I think the whole idea of researchers truly helping reporters become better information consumers and users is going to be a big role, and it's going to be requiring a lot more interaction than they had in the past.

One final question. Everything's speeding up. We have this challenge of real-time news and the Internet increasing the urgency of news, with news being 24/7 and constant deadlines. What does that do to researchers and reporters—make them crazy?

Yes. Again, it goes back to my point that it's not the hardware and software that are the problem. It's the people and the system, and in a lot of ways this is requiring a rethinking of what kind of journalism you're trying to practice each day. I don't think that there is complete clarity yet on just what that is. Are you going to try to be all types of news to all types of people? Or are you going to have the niche that you are going to be identified as providing? That's the real challenge to inventing a future.

Super Searcher Power Tips

➤ My main advice for researchers and reporters is to think very small about the Internet. If you feel that you have to know all of it to know any of it, you're doomed.

➤ You can click on "cache" in the corresponding entry in your results list and Google will retrieve the page as it was when it was spidered by Google. So, Google can be used to track a disappearing URL.

➤ I think one of the biggest shifts for people in approaching information on the Internet is how to move away from "clip-file heading" thinking. People who still approach research in terms of the "subject heading" are going to quickly be swamped. The most important thing is to think of the task first.

➤ To me, that's the most important first step, to be very clear about what you're really trying to locate. The next thing is to know the differences between the different kinds of Web locating tools—and the value of a Yahoo!-type directory if all you need is a couple of good Web sites.

➤ The alert services will capture and tell you about the very kinds of things that you won't be able to find in most of the major search sites. Search sites that rely on a spider or robot software to go out and index the Web sites may only send the robot out once every six weeks. So the new information, the stuff that's fresh, the stuff that's really going to be good news tips, will not be picked up by a search-site spider.

➤ What is fascinating for the potential of doing new kinds of journalism is the ability to get at a lot of "agendas" very quickly. So, there may be less black-and-white reporting and more shades of gray, which I think can only improve the journalism that we do.

Timothy K. Maloy

Reporter, New Media Professor, and Internet Guru

T.K. Maloy is the author of The Internet Research Guide and editor of *The Internet Newsroom,* a newsletter for journalists and information professionals. He teaches new media courses at American University in Washington, DC.

tkmaloy@editors-service.com
www.editors-service.com

How did you get into news research?

I come from a very standard print journalism background. I started out as a small-town reporter. The skills I bring to researching, whether online or offline, I learned as a reporter. I want to emphasize how reporters are much like any other information professional. I did not realize this until years later. But a young reporter, a cub reporter, is trained in a certain set of newsroom research folkways by editors and other people in the newsroom. I learned that way, without knowing it, how to gather information in an orderly and organized fashion. This includes what's known as primary-source research, which for reporters simply means interviewing people, and doing research in a library. Then, several years ago, journalists started to use online databases, and now we use the Internet and its World Wide Web quite habitually.

When you were a reporter, did you use online resources, and did you use the library?

Yes, I used both. Small-town newspapers usually have some-body acting as a part-time news librarian, a person who can prove very helpful to research. Working in collaboration with them, I would do research through services such as Lexis-Nexis [106, see Appendix]. Small-town newspapers do not have quite as sophisticated news library centers as you get in a large metro daily. I still consider myself a journalist, a reporter, and a researcher. The larger the news organization I have worked with, usually the better the research capability. It was not standard for each reporter to have desktop access to online databases, but no matter where I have worked, I usually have collaborated with news librarians to search Lexis-Nexis, Dialog [44], Dow Jones [48], Westlaw [202], and other database services.

In those days, reporters actually worked as a team with their librarian researchers.

Yes, and I believe that's still the case. You refer to "those days," but I would say that reporters are still getting used to online research and, whether it's the Internet or an online database, it's become more familiar to reporters only in the last five years, at most. A lot of reporters have just started doing more electronic research, and computer-aided research and analysis, in general.

Are you proficient on the traditional search systems like Dialog and Lexis-Nexis?

I am proficient to a degree with Lexis-Nexis, though not as much as the average news librarian. I would recommend to any-one who uses any of the online databases that they get a tutorial from a librarian. This can include lessons in simple Boolean syn-tax and commands to refine your search—delimiters and so on—so you can limit the time scope and the focus of your search. I'm also familiar with using Bloomberg [25], which is a great financial news and information database.

I know you're not doing reporting for major newspapers at this point, but do you still use some of those other search systems along with the Internet for research?

I do use them, and occasionally I do reporting for larger organizations. I just did an on-air piece for MSNBC [125] about Internet sweepstakes and a piece about online voting. Most of my research for that was done using the Internet, because I was writing about something involving the Internet. But I still often rely on databases outside of the Net. I rely heavily on Lexis-Nexis to do a broad literature search, particularly a news database search, to make sure I'm not missing anything.

The Net is good for news searching as well, but services like Lexis-Nexis or Dow Jones excel for doing keyword searching. It's hard to do a keyword search on the Internet that just looks for news articles, for instance. I can't go onto the Internet and say, "I want all the news articles about the Internet in the last year." That's where Lexis-Nexis is much more orderly than the Internet. You have a give-and-take that works better for research.

Certainly, the powerful search capabilities and refinements that the online systems have, as opposed to a search engine on the Internet, make them more attractive.

Exactly. You have greater control of your search and your search strategy, and therefore I like to think that the results are better. However, it depends on what you're doing. The Internet is certainly an excellent source of material for the lay person and a great first line of research for almost any occasion. But for an orderly search, sometimes the databases should be your final resort, depending on whether you're trying to produce a research report, a news story, or a book.

How do you generally build a search? When would you start an search on the Internet versus a commercial database?

I start searching on the Internet because the Internet is excellent at what I call open-source searching. That's a term from the intelligence field meaning information that's a matter of public record, both current and historical. The Internet is great for a broad category search. I start with a very simple search, what I call a serendipity search. I enter a single keyword or set of keywords, and simply take a look at the results. Searching on the Internet is improving rapidly. I can quickly ascertain whether the sources are yielding results that are good, accurate, and answer the question. Using the Internet can be very quick. If the results of your initial search are not satisfactory, you can go back and quickly refine your search methods.

At that point you can start to become more sophisticated in your Internet searching—what you referred to as building your search. Whether you're using Lexis-Nexis or a search engine like AltaVista [7], you can use many of the same Boolean syntaxes to narrow things down. AltaVista Advanced [8] offers a number of sophisticated search techniques that you can use.

Is AltaVista one of your preferred search engines?

I would say that AltaVista is the top engine on the strength of its database and its sophisticated search capabilities and commands. According to my research, as well as AltaVista's own reports and outside auditors, it has one of the largest databases of Web documents. As of the end of 1999, the Web was cited as having over a billion pages of documents, which is an impressive database. AltaVista encompasses part of that—not all of it, by any means. But it has one of the largest databases, and one of the best interfaces for advanced searching. I also recommend Northern Light [140].

I was going to say that recent studies have shown that Northern Light is edging above all the other engines in its coverage.

That may well be so. The different search engines always strive to have larger databases, because one of their selling points is how much of the Internet they encompass. Contrary to popular belief and some search engine claims, they do not encompass as much as we might think.

Northern Light is an excellent engine as well. It is neck and neck with AltaVista in the sophistication of the searching you can do. And jumping from what you were talking about earlier, about using databases other than the Internet, Northern Light is a hybrid, in that it bridges the Internet and the database world. They have a proprietary database, supplementing the World Wide Web materials, that you can delve into for a very low fee. They also have a variety of mini-search capabilities—for instance, you can search for just government data. To me it's a very orderly search engine compared to the others. It literally organizes your searches into topical folders, which I find very useful.

Let's go back to building a search. You talked about quickly assessing the results from a search engine and then refining it.

I already have in mind some more refined search strategy, but I like to do my serendipity search first, just to see what the possible results are—particularly in finding sources that I might not have expected.

After using a broad search engine such as AltaVista, you might want to go to specialized search engines. You might want to go to FedStats [64], for instance, if you're looking for items within the purview of the U.S. government and federal statistics. Some searchers prefer to start out with the narrowest search strategy possible and then broaden out. For me, a good search usually starts out broad and narrows down into the types of tools I use and the types of sources that I employ, including individual Web sites that my broad search might have turned up.

Using the example of government data, you might be looking for U.S. legislative information. Let's say I put the word "abortion" into a search engine. That's a hot-button category; I'll see what that turns up. I might want to know more about abortion legislation, choice advocacy, and what some of the arguments and controversies are about the issue. So, first, I'll do my broad search. But then I'll go to a Web site such as Thomas, the Library of Congress Web site [174]. There I can get specific legislation. Then I might go to the Supreme Court Web site [196], or to one of the good legal Web sites, such as Cornell University's [36]. I start out broad and see what that reveals, and then I narrow it down into specific sources of information on an issue or topic.

With the search engines covering an increasingly broad range of sources, the risk has always been that you retrieve so much information that it's actually meaningless. How do you deal with that?

That is a problem. An average broad search can yield anywhere from fifty thousand to five hundred thousand hits, which is much more material than you can reasonably go through and analyze. I suggest going rapidly through the first several hundred results, bringing your information skills to bear. You quickly look at the results and analyze them. Assess whether these are sources of information that could be accurate and useful. That's one of the great issues that impacts researchers—whether the information is accurate, timely, and unbiased.

What advice do you give on determining accuracy and integrity?

The classic advice is first to consider the source. If the information source is established and well-known—*The Wall Street Journal,* or a government agency, for example—by and large, you can believe—unless you are, perhaps, a government conspiracist—that the information has some degree of accuracy. It's gone through a process of review before being published on the Internet. Peer-reviewed journals can also be considered accurate sources of information.

Not that individual publishing efforts on the Internet should automatically be suspect, but when something has obviously been published by an individual who lacks an organizational affiliation, then you have to treat it as such, and bear in mind that it has not gone through any kind of editorial process before it appeared online. Individual publishing efforts can range from the highly accurate to the highly questionable—say, Holocaust revisionism and things that obviously don't have any foundation in fact.

Have you personally found source integrity to be a problem in your research?

I have not. To me it's usually apparent when something does not have any organizational editorship behind it. You can go to a university history department and find academic papers published by professors. Those I would consider good sources of information. But, using an analogy of straying from one room to another, in that same university history department you might come upon individual publications done by students, which might lack the accuracy of the professors' work. Again, it's just a simple criterion: What is the source of the information? What is its organizational background?

The problem with the Internet, for the lay person doing research, is that anything that appears in print automatically gains a certain kind of credibility. The Internet is a print text medium. Items published on the Internet gain the authority of the printed word. Again, I don't encounter a great many problems in separating the wheat from the chaff.

But I'll bet you have to tell your students.

Yes, we have to help guide other people through this. Some of the medical Web sites have excellent information in terms of background information on medical conditions and histories and so forth. But when we mention the Web, we mustn't forget the other parts of the Internet—the Usenet newsgroups, the various chat groups and discussion forums, mailing lists, advice columns, and so on. It's when you get into those areas of the Internet that you have to suggest a rule of *caveat emptor—* "buyer beware." I would not suggest that a person take medical advice gained from the Internet that's given by anyone other than a physician, for obvious reasons. But that's the nature of information online and offline as well—you can go into a bookstore and buy a book that might not have the best advice.

You mentioned online mailing lists and forums. How do you personally use them and how would you recommend news researchers take advantage of these?

I do not use them as much as I did initially, because it has become much harder to gain some order out of the increasing clutter, the background noise, of the newsgroups. But they can be very useful, particularly for journalists, because of their topical nature. Liszt [111] is good for finding a topical newsgroup. If you are looking for an expert or for a quote on a topic, newsgroups are an excellent source. Usually, introducing yourself as a reporter will quickly yield a quote from somebody. They're also useful for quickly learning about a topic by listening in on the debate and the exchange of information. It can be a specialized topic, such as metallurgy or rocket science, or something more mundane, such as bird-watching. Some people refer to newsgroups as the public square of the Internet, and that's an apt analogy.

One of my top searching tips is to use a beat approach to information gathering, where you divide news into specific subject categories. An important part of reporting often involves doing what's done in the street beat, where you interview the man and woman on the street. That's where the newsgroups and mailing lists are very useful—for getting public opinion very quickly.

The beat approach sounds intriguing. Can you give me an example of how it works?

The average reporter, whether a small-town or a major metro reporter, usually divides the day and the work into a topical set of categories. This is known in journalism parlance as working your beat. Literally, physically, you go to city hall, you go to police headquarters, to the school board, and so on. Then you might go to the local Chamber of Commerce to get business information, or to a large local corporation. You physically go to these places, and that's where you talk to people or access public records. In terms of topical categories, city hall is obviously the topic "government," school board is the topic "education," Chamber of Commerce is "business," and police headquarters is "crime and judiciary." The beat approach to research enables you to organize your information gathering, whether it's online or offline, into logical topic categories.

It's similar to the principle used by the average person when they bookmark Web sites. They're developing a regular set of stopping places on the Internet where they gain information. To me that is a very good approach. The good and bad of the Internet is its size and the amount of data. Whether it's the top ten spots or the top two hundred that have topical relevance to you, bookmarking acts as a way to order your information. You just have to exercise the daily discipline of going and gathering information from those spots to keep yourself current. That's why I recommend the beat approach. It's simply a method of organizing your information gathering.

Nora Paul talks about moving away from "clip-file heading" thinking and, instead, thinking about the task. It seems to me that you're saying the same thing—the task is go to city hall or go to police headquarters, not just throw the term into a search engine.

I always agree completely with Nora! It *is* a task-oriented thing. It goes back to our discussion about building a search strategy. You do undertake a task when you're searching: Are you looking for government information? Are you looking for criminal information? That is exactly the nature of a beat.

Let's go on to some of your other favorite tips.

The challenge in searching, whether online or offline, is the amount of information we have to deal with. So the real task is how to simplify what we do. We need to have a really simple set of tips.

One of my favorite techniques is to use a "bot," which is short for robot. You have an online agent, as it were, that does your information bidding for you. It is much like using a search engine, where you put in a keyword or a set of delimiters, and so forth.

Many people are already using bots and they don't even realize it. A great example is the *San Jose Mercury News'* [161] News Hound, which was an automated clipping service. News Hound is an apt metaphor, since it's like sending a dog out to fetch a bone. With News Hound, you put in a set of information categories and it then brought clippings back for you. I used it on occasion with very successful results. It's the equivalent of using something like Lexis-Nexis to build a clipping file. Excite NewsTracker [58] and Wired's NewsBot [135] work much the same way.

Beyond these public bots available to anyone on the Internet are specialized bots that you can run from your desktop. The one I'll cite as an example is Intelliseek's BullsEye [250]. This is automated robot searching software that you can set out upon the Net at night, for instance, while you're asleep, or any other time when you might be doing another task. You launch it from your desktop. It goes out on the Net; it might spend a minute or half an hour there. It brings back a comprehensive set of search results. So, using bots is a good way to simplify the task of searching. They are automated and can undertake the searching for you while you are working on other tasks.

When comparable information is available in a number of different places, how do you decide where to access it?

An interesting question. For instance, do I want to go to Yahoo! News [209], which is an excellent aggregator of news? Or, if I'm looking for financial news specifically, why don't I go directly to where I can get that financial news? I might want to go right to CBS MarketWatch.com [30] or Wall Street Journal Interactive [197]. In the case of *The Wall Street Journal* site, although you pay a nominal annual fee, you get the entirety of the Dow Jones financial database, which is behind *The Wall Street Journal*. You can search *The Wall Street Journal* content and get company background information as well. You might pick up much of the same information in business articles at sites throughout the Net, but there are some advantages to going straight to the source—and sometimes to a fee-based source.

If you're doing primary-source research—for instance, looking for information about Ford Motors or Ford cars—you might want to actually go to the Ford Motors Web site, not just look through news clippings and financial reporting about Ford. Increasingly, corporations are seeing the Web as a great way to "disintermediate." They can get their information straight out to the public. That's good for researchers in that it increases the amount of primary-source materials. Again, you have to "consider the source" when you're going straight to the corporation for information. But it's still a great source of unfiltered data.

Other than going to all those individual sites for corporate press releases, who are the best aggregators of press releases?

As a reporter, I regularly use PR Newswire [147]. It excels in searching for company information, because you can put in the company name and bring up press releases for the last year. PR Newswire also has a news email service called NewsDesk, which is industry sector-related rather than by company. They bought

ProfNet [148], which delivers expert commentary on your individual query through its network of experts.

For company information I also like the Securities and Exchange Commission site, sec.gov [194]. You can fill out a variety of online forms to be apprised in email alerts of events that might be relevant to your information specialty. You can ask for notification when a particular company files a 10-K, for instance.

I've found the financial and business area on Yahoo! to be very helpful for that, linking me not only to PR Newswire, BusinessWire, and Reuters, but also highlighting some SEC filings.

I've got to agree. At one time it was considered somewhat scandalous to recommend Yahoo! because it was the plain vanilla place to go for topical-directory searches. But they have kept up very well in terms of categorizing and aggregating information. Yahoo! is really an excellent place to start for news searches, for business backgrounds, and so on.

How did you build your personal list of bookmarks, which I'm sure must be extensive?

Again, I use the beat approach. I often tell people, as a short explanation of my profession, that I'm a technology journalist. A great deal of my research deals with the Internet itself, so I have a number of categories such as new technologies, new search engines, and so forth. I've developed a tech beat where I follow the Internet using news sites such as CNET [33] or ZDNet [211], and going straight to a lot of the computer-oriented Web sites to see what the new technologies are.

We've talked about searching and about organizing your research. Let's talk now about output. How do you handle the data that you get and want to save

for later? Do you print some things out, or save and organize it on your hard drive?

One of my favorite tips is to use personal information managers (PIMs). PIMs are software packages that are designed to combine Internet retrieval with indexing and retrieval of information on your PC desktop and in your document files. PIMs do multi-source searching, helping you find things that are inside your PC and also out on the Net. They take a while to get used to, and some people think they just add another layer of complexity in terms of information searching. But they can prove very useful for people in the news and business world.

A good one is Enfish Tracker Pro [248]. It cross-references information in much the same way as an old-fashioned card catalog. You enter keywords, both names and topics, in the software index, and the program cross-references for you. When you click a topic it will search across Web sites that you have saved, or sites in your bookmark file, or through your email or your document files.

I have to admit that I am old-fashioned because I print out a great deal from the Internet as well. I print out Web pages and pull quotes and background information from them. Of course, because you are writing most output electronically, it's great to be able to lift quotes straight off the Internet. You can clip the URLs and cite them in your reference section if you're writing a research paper, or for a news article where you want to reference the information. I've learned to operate seamlessly, gathering information from the Internet and plugging it straight into my product. Of course, I want to avoid the crime of plagiarism—I'm suggesting *selective* quoting, and citing the origin of that information.

Thinking about the amount of information available now on the Net, can you give me some examples of things you can now find online that were not obtainable before?

The obvious growth area on the Internet is in the dot-com arena. While it is not of relevance to some researchers, certainly a great deal of commercial information exists on the Internet for the "shopping researcher." This can prove useful in a number of ways. Whether you're searching for computer hardware, or you want to get the lowest price on a potpie, it's very handy for the consumer researcher.

At the other end of the information spectrum, because the Net is a relatively new information medium, there has not been a lot of historical data on the Internet. If you want to read newspapers from the last century, the Internet has not been a good medium for research. It is getting better, since a lot of human history is being digitized now. Libraries and other entities are putting a lot of historical and archival data online, including old documents, newspapers, and other artifacts. Project Gutenberg [150] continues its long and useful labor to put the world's books online, the classics that are in the public domain. I think that's very heartening for researchers and teachers, and it's great for students.

Government information from around the world is increasing. United States government information has come online fairly comprehensively within the last two to three years. In terms of global data, more and more world governments are going online. That's a good thing for the spread of democracy and for access to world information, and quite significant for news researchers.

Academic departments are going global, too. It's heartening to see the amount of academic publishing that's going on in Sri Lanka, for instance, and other developing countries. This is a great thing for academics in the developing world—and elsewhere—who can now share information with each other. So we are starting to see more global, more academic, more historical, and more commercial information on the Net.

Do you have a favorite example of a research project that was particularly challenging or fun to do?

My specialty is writing about the Internet itself and the resources that are available on the Internet. It can take a while to compile a comprehensive list of what exists. One of my favorite stories—now about two years old—was on art resources on the Net. I went to all the great galleries around the world that had an online, virtual presence. To me, it was sublime to see everything from the Mona Lisa to the Pyramids of Egypt to the Vatican Library online. It was very interesting to research, but it also took quite a while.

But I found some great artistic metasites such as Art Museum.Net [15] and Artnet.com [16]. That's another method of searching—you try to find a meta- or comprehensive topical directory in the area you're researching, and from there you can find the specific items you're looking for. In this instance, I went from an art metasite to specific Web locales, such as the Met in New York [122], or the Louvre in France [112], or the Tate in London [172], and so forth.

This particular article about art resources also demonstrates the multimedia capabilities of the Internet. That's certainly a departure from, say, Lexis-Nexis, where you do not get any multimedia.

I'm guessing that the art project was done for your *Internet Newsroom*. Can you tell me a bit about what that is and how you aim to help journalists with it?

Yes, it was. *The Internet Newsroom* [97] is a hardcopy publication—with a companion Web site—that deals with the specific topic of researching on the Internet. It was originally launched for my fellow news researchers, people in the journalism profession who were starting to use the Net three or four years ago. We simply would talk about Web sites that were topical or relevant for those in the news profession—politics, government information, and so on.

Although it started out for journalists, we since have gained many other subscribers among corporate librarians, students, and journalism departments. I think it's useful as a hardcopy newsletter because of the "less is more" formula. Yes, you can go onto Yahoo! and the search engines and so on, but we like to think that we do the searching for our readers, so it saves them time. We might spend ten or twenty hours on any given article, looking through sites that we deem to be the most useful for a topic, and then we choose the top sites.

What do you like best about what you do?

I come from a print press background where what I did was always very eclectic. That's still what I enjoy most about writing and journalism—being eclectic, inquiring, and able to stick my nose in just about everything. My interest in the Internet is above and beyond the technology of the Internet. It's what's *inside* the Internet, which has really become as large as the world itself in terms of the amount of information and the type of information that is available.

Any given story that I'm writing will take me around the virtual world. It's like covering a very large waterfront. I never fail to be surprised by the Internet and the new phenomena that I come across, whether it's new technology or new research resources.

What do you find most frustrating about the Net?

The problem we will continue to struggle with is the sheer volume of information. The information output in the world today is so great that the average person born today could not, over the span of an entire lifetime, read the amount of material put out in one day. The sociologist Alvin Toffler wrote about this a number of years ago in his book, *Future Shock*. That is the problem that exists now on the Net, and with information in general.

In future searching, I think we will see more intelligence seeking and so-called data mining. Data mining will use intelligent searching software, which will help bring order and meaning out of text and multimedia documents and raw data.

Super Searcher Power Tips

➤ I like to do a broad "serendipity search" first, just to see what the possible results are—particularly in finding sources that I might not have expected.

➤ If you are looking for an expert or for a quote on a topic, newsgroups are an excellent source of information. Usually, introducing yourself as a reporter will quickly yield a quote from somebody. Newsgroups are also useful for quickly learning about a topic by listening in on the debate and the exchange of information.

➤ The beat approach to research enables you to organize your information gathering, whether it's online or offline, into logical topic categories.

➤ Using bots like News Hound and BullsEye is a good way to simplify the task of searching. These automated agents can undertake the searching for you while you are working on other tasks.

➤ Personal information managers (PIMs) help you find things that are inside your PC and also out on the Net. A good one is Enfish Tracker Pro. It cross-references information in much the same way as an old-fashioned card catalog.

Duff Wilson

Hard-Hitting Investigative Reporter and Webmaster

Duff Wilson is a longtime journalist and award-winning reporter for *The Seattle Times,* where he was a finalist for the 1998 Pulitzer Prize for Public Service. He is also Webmaster for his own site, the Reporter's Desktop.

dwilson@seattletimes.com
www.reporter.org/desktop
www.seattletimes.com

Tell me a bit about your background and how you came to *The Seattle Times.*

I'm from a newspaper family that published a weekly newspaper in a small town, so journalism runs in my blood. I've been writing since I was about twelve or thirteen. I went through an undergraduate school in Washington state, and then to Columbia University Graduate School of Journalism. I've been in Seattle for most of my career, though I spent two years in Washington, DC.

How did you get into researching? Do you use news librarians to assist you or do you prefer to do research yourself?

Librarians' work is helpful but I do a lot of it myself. For instance, I started researching laws and court rulings to apply standards to subjects that I wrote about. So I spent time in law libraries. Now I spend that time on the Web at FindLaw.com [67, see Appendix]. I'm always inclined to do in-depth investigative articles that involve a lot of research.

Have you used some of the traditional services such as Lexis-Nexis or Dow Jones?

I did learn Lexis-Nexis [106]. That is an example of where I would often turn to the newspaper's librarians to pull articles because they were better at it. I do the in-person research at government offices, business offices, and on the street, but I use the news librarians here at *The Seattle Times*, especially for Lexis-Nexis. But now, since the Web's opened up so much, I do most of the detailed research myself. The problem is not a lack of information. It's information overload.

How did you become comfortable with doing Net research? How did you get up to speed?

It wasn't that long ago that the Net was kind of an exotic, cutting-edge tool for reporters, almost as if doing Internet research was computer-assisted reporting. I think that's a misnomer. It would be like saying "telephone-assisted reporting." To me, computer-assisted reporting is work that involves original analysis of data. Researching subjects or using the Internet to find information is like using the telephone or your feet to walk down to the library. It's no longer exotic. Everyone has to do it. I learned to use computers in the punch-card days of IBM mainframes. I learned to use the Net from coworkers and instructors at Investigative Reporters and Editors (IRE) [99] and the National Institute for Computer-Assisted Reporting (NICAR) [129]. Now I try to keep up to speed on my own and with help from people who use the Reporter's Desktop [157], and publications like Danny Sullivan's Search Engine Watch [221], and books and magazines.

What kinds of information searching do you do?

My research needs vary all the time. I research anything from laws to scientific studies to other news articles. We have a group of reporters that does special projects—in-depth reports on any-thing that seems especially important. It could be breaking news or, as it often is, a subject of some importance that hasn't been adequately covered. We have a broad mandate to cover the city and the region. The Reporter's Desktop on the Web shows the kinds of research I do. It covers the gamut from phone books to law libraries.

Let's talk about your Reporter's Desktop. How did that evolve? Was it a personal list that you then decided to make available to reporter friends?

Yes, that's exactly right. It evolved from bookmarks. About five or six years ago, I found a site on the Web where I could build a little home page with ten bookmarks, free. I think it was the GeoCities [208] Web site. Then I looked at the HTML coding behind that and realized how easy it would be to not limit it to ten, but to copy and paste the source code and go to twenty or thirty. That's when I started to learn HTML, by studying the source code behind it, learning how to actually copy and paste and revise larger amounts of code. I learned how to insert search boxes with push buttons and graphics. I began to borrow from a lot of Web sites to build a home page for my own work that would include forms to fill in. I wanted not just the links, but the forms, so that I could get information with a single click instead of going to a bookmarked link and then having to find the form to fill in. I eliminated the middle click.

It was initially to save myself time, and it still is. New resources that I use a lot, I put on the Reporter's Desktop. Other people suggest improvements. I test them out. I try to keep it short, though. It always has to be short and fast—that's the key. It's not a mega- or comprehensive bookmark site. It's supposed to be built for speed. I use it for everyday work, for phone numbers, driving directions, as well as the overall Web searches and spe-cialized search engines and so on.

It's all free, all on the public Web. You just have to know where to look. I began to share what I'd found with some people because they were stumbling around the Web like I was doing years ago. And they liked it. Eventually I've shared the desktop with other newspapers and professional groups across the country, and taught it at IRE and NICAR and the Poynter Institute [146]. Then IRE sponsored the site as a noncommercial, cooperative venture. Now, a lot of other reporters and editors across the country use it as a home page, too.

It's very nicely done. Do your librarians get involved working with reporters, teaching research techniques or use of the Internet, or helping with bookmarks?

Definitely. The librarians are very helpful. We have a top-notch library that I've worked with a lot. We have one of the best intranets that I've seen, if not the best one in the country, for newspaper use. It's called *The Seattle Times* Java Café. It has tools like instant look-up on drivers' licenses, voter registrations, payroll data, real estate ownership, campaign contributions. We can find out all that on our intranet here at the newspaper in a couple of clicks.

We've got a top-notch library staff here. And they do more of this than I do, working with other reporters. I just happen to have developed a Reporter's Desktop on the outer Web that I try to keep current. The research library helps me. People from across the country help. I get two or three emails a week from people suggesting new sites, and I'm very selective in these, because I don't want to clutter up the site with little-used bookmarks. People can, and should, keep their own specialized bookmarks. I intend for the Desktop to include tools that most everyone can use fairly frequently. It supplements the more detailed work that research librarians do.

Who chooses what goes on your intranet?
As reporters gather information, or tips,
or places to go for specific things, do they
contribute to the intranet so that you're
sharing among each other?

There's some of that; I'd like to see more sharing. The group that decides what goes on the intranet is led by our chief librarian, Tom Boyer. He started computer-assisted reporting at the Norfolk *Virginian-Pilot* in the early '90s. We have a staff of about seven Web-savvy research librarians. They're constantly importing data from government agencies and making new links to commercial CDs we buy. We currently have driver's licenses, voter registration, payrolls, property holdings, campaign contributions, and business licenses on our intranet.

I do think it would be better to involve reporters more. For instance, we're trying to set up a page on the intranet for reporters to share news tips and leads. We get a lot of phone calls that perhaps one reporter can't follow but another could. On another page on the intranet, I'm setting up a list of the best places to find public records on people and companies in this state—all the places reporters have to go. Both pages will have interactive features. If you have a tip, or a source for public records, or a better phone number for an important contact, you'll be able to share it on the intranet.

That sounds excellent. Do you sometimes
encounter reporters who are resistant to
sharing? Maybe they want to keep the scoop
for themselves?

I don't put *my* best sources out there. I have to protect them. Reporters naturally try to keep the best tips for themselves. But what's not top priority with one reporter may be a hit with another.

Do you work as teams on large projects, such as several reporters with an editor, and a librarian assigned as a researcher?

Yes, we frequently do; I'm on two such teams now. The reporters will be conducting an investigation, and we're assigned one of the news librarians to call on at any time for research, including finding and printing out court dockets, Web research, and setting up databases. We have not only a news librarian, but also a director of computer-assisted reporting who sits near us and who is especially good at relational databases. The computer-assisted reporting person, David Heath, will call government agencies and get data from them directly. He's great at talking them down on the price and getting them to release more information. So, on both of the project teams I'm on right now, there are two reporters, the director of computer-assisted reporting, and one news librarian. We have access to a second librarian as needed. So, really, more than half the team are people who specialize in news research.

Is this new, this model of putting together teams that involve researchers, reporters, and editors? Has this evolved because of increasing access to Internet resources?

Yes, I think so, not just because of the Internet, but because of the importance of computer-assisted reporting in general. The technology moves so fast that it is impossible for most reporters to keep up with it. So there's specialization. It's important to call on specialists in computer-assisted reporting, news research, reporting, writing, and editing. I used to do a lot of database work with Rbase, dBase, and Paradox, and now with Access [252], and I just can't keep up with the changes. It's nice to have somebody to call on who knows the latest. I think that's why the team approach is so important.

Information on the Net has certainly grown dramatically. How have your searching methods changed? When do you still use a professional online service and when and how do you use Web resources?

Lexis-Nexis Universe [107] is on the Web now, and it's a lot easier to use than the old Lexis-Nexis. But so much is available on the Web that I find myself turning to Lexis-Nexis less and less. So much is on the Web for free. Excite's NewsTracker [59], for instance, is a free personal clipping service. It lets you type in search terms for any topic. You can choose whether the article must, or must not, or may contain that term. Then it searches the Web and delivers weekly or daily pointers to articles on a site accessible only to you. It searches more than 300 online newspapers and magazines that are available free on the Web. It's basically an alert service so that I can see what other significant media across the country and around the world are doing on the topic. So often in reporting, you have to become an instant expert on something that you know nothing about. That's where a service like NewsTracker is invaluable. You can get up to speed in a short time.

Have you any other special news sources or email alert services that you find particularly useful?

There's also TotalNEWS [177] and Yahoo! Alerts [207], which are similar to the NewsTracker service, but I haven't used them as much. I use Northern Light [140] a lot because it not only covers the free Web, but it also has special collections of documents that would be similar to the pay-per-view documents you get in Lexis-Nexis. It is reasonably priced, about two dollars per document.

When information is available in a number of different places, how do you decide where to

access it? Is it price? Or is it the ability to search in a certain way?

It's speed and accuracy, not price. Overload is the problem. I took a year off recently to write a book, and I hired a researcher to help me. She did wonderful Web research, but there was so much of it that it just buried me. The problem with all this is how to be selective. I often just go to Yahoo! [206] as a starting point, or I go to Google [80], a search engine that uses popularity ranking for Web sites. They help me focus and simplify and understand.

So you find classified directories like Yahoo! very useful. Do you use any of the metasearch engines?

I have tried them but I don't use the metasearch engines much. I've also tried software products like Copernic [247], Symantec's Internet FastFind [251], and WebRecord Research Pro [255], but I think they're too much trouble. There are great metasearch engines like MetaCrawler [120], InferenceFind [91], and Dogpile [47], but I find they overload me. I find that Google, Yahoo!, and Northern Light work just fine without having to search through ten or fifteen different engines. I get plenty with the single engines. If I don't find what I need and want, I'll go to a second or third or fourth search engine. That's one thing about the Reporter's Desktop page; it's easy to bounce from engine to engine. I've included the metasearch sites Inference Find, MetaCrawler, The BigHub [24], Dogpile, and ProFusion [149], which people like. They're on the page, but I don't use them very often. If I needed to find something very small and specific, I would use HotBot [86].

How do you keep up?

Danny Sullivan's Search Engine Watch is the main way I keep up on the innovations in search engine technology. And I hear on a regular basis from fifteen or twenty journalists and researchers from across the country who suggest new or improved versions of sites I already have on the Desktop.

So, in fact, by putting out the Reporter's Desktop for other people, you've ensured that they will give you back the best of their suggestions to improve the site.

Exactly. We don't want to waste our time with something that's not the best, right? For instance, we were talking about the news search engines, the ones that specialize in searching newspapers and magazines. I don't want to include all fifteen or twenty of them, or however many there might be, on the Desktop. I want to have the best one or two. Maybe I don't need them, but as I hear about the others, such as NewsTrawler [138], NewsBot [135], and NewsHub [136], I'll check them out and compare them to NewsTracker, 1stHeadlines [3], and TotalNEWS, which I have on the Desktop. And, if any seem significantly better, I'll include those and try to cut something that's not as useful.

Have you used electronic mailing lists or discussions to tap into topics that you're reporting on, or to find people to talk to?

I can always do that. I'll find online sources through Deja.com [42] or Liszt [111]. They're very valid modes for finding experts, especially in science, for finding anecdotes, and finding people that I can call and talk to. I was doing a story four or five years ago on the "gray market" of information, focusing on information brokers. That was an interesting one because I started that reporting on the Web by joining a discussion group of information brokers who were mostly private investigators. Then I asked them for examples of gray market information—medical records, unlisted phone numbers, bank records, that sort of thing—and pretty soon I was getting good leads, some good sources, people to talk to … and I also got kicked off the list. They had some idea that what they were doing was off the record, though the list didn't say it was off the record. I think everything on the Web is pretty much on the record.

Generally, I don't have the time or patience to keep up with discussion groups on any given subject. Maybe there are some good mailing lists, but the journalism and investigative reporting lists that I've been on in the past are so full of noise that they are ultimately counterproductive. I tap into specialized mailing lists on a project-by-project basis.

How do you deal with data integrity and authority of material that you find on the Net? Any tips for evaluating your sources and sites? Has that been a problem for you?

It's a problem that I worry about but I haven't been burned on yet. Government sites probably have the most integrity. If you go one step away, to a nonprofit or advocacy group that's using government data, such as The Right-to-Know Network [160], it may seem credible but I'd follow up before relying on the information. I would need a live person. If I'm using information I've gotten from somebody by email, I always call to verify who I'm talking to. One of my pet peeves about Web sites is that many of them don't have phone numbers on them. You know there's somebody behind it, but it takes a long time to track them down.

On data integrity in the business realm, of course, the Securities and Exchange Commission records online through EDGAR [52] can be relied on as much as paper documents. My second favorite site for business information is Hoover's Online [85] because it provides a quick corporate snapshot, links to news articles, officers, and financial data. I take that with a little more salt than the SEC site, because I don't know who has written that description.

When you begin research for an article, where do you start? Do you have a general method for your searching?

I start with Google or Yahoo! or Northern Light. I check Hoover's and EDGAR and Thomas [174], if they apply. I'll get clips from Lexis-Nexis. It depends on the subject. I try to cast a wide net, and I start early with a chronology and a telephone list. I'm always looking for roadmap sources, experts who can steer me in the right direction. And I'm also looking for whistleblowers.

What do you find you can get on the Net that a few years ago you couldn't get at all?

There's so much. I love the mapping programs like MapBlast [116] and MapQuest [117]. You can type in two street addresses, and it gives you step-by-step directions, door to door. The best reverse phone directory is on the Web now from AnyWho [13]. If you have someone's phone number, you can type that in and get their name and address. There's a private vendor who sells a phone disk with a reverse directory, but it's incomplete and out of date compared to the free version on the Web. I also use the reverse email directory on InfoSpace [94], but it's incomplete. You can easily change an email address. Sometimes, though, with just somebody's email address, I can find out a lot about them and what their phone number is if I don't already have it.

I used to have to go to the law library to find lawyers that specialized in a certain area. Now with the Martindale-Hubbell [118] directory online, they're easy to find. Same with the American Medical Association [12] Web site for finding doctors.

Two of my very favorite sites that I use all the time are MED-LINE [119] for medical and scientific questions and experts, and the Encyclopaedia Britannica [53], which is now available free on the Web for a thirty-day trial, and then by subscription for only five dollars a month.

Tell me about a favorite news project that you worked on, one that was particularly challenging or fun from a research perspective.

I think my favorite was my series of articles for *The Seattle Times* in 1997 that exposed how heavy industry saved money disposing of hazardous wastes by mixing them into fertilizer. The waste would have some fertilizer value, such as zinc, but a lot of contaminants, such as cadmium, lead, and dioxins. I heard about this from the mayor of a small town here and I just found it unbelievable—preposterous—that it could happen.

But, using the Web and email, as well as phone calls and interviews and freedom-of-information requests for public records, I found documents that were basically hidden in plain sight that corroborated it. On the Web, I found places called industrial material exchanges, where people with industrial waste to dispose of listed it in order to find people who would take it—like a blind-dating service on the Web. I found a company on the Web called CoZinCo that was publishing chemical analyses of different products showing high amounts of toxic lead. They were blowing the whistle on the Web. Of course, I got a lot of scientific information on MEDLINE, too. I used the Web as my medical library, agronomist, biologist, toxicologist, lawyer, and telephone operator. Just a couple of years ago, I would have had to sit and thumb through registers in government offices because none of this was posted online. And I wouldn't have had the ability to find out easily what was going on in Canada, Australia, and Europe.

I used email on this project to keep in touch with scientists and government officials around the world. As I was developing the information, I built an email list that became essential to my work. I would use it to raise questions and get reality checks. Then, when my articles began to come out in the newspaper, I would send these people the articles by email and get their immediate feedback. Literally, I could change or improve an article between the first and second edition of the same day's newspaper. There were more than twenty articles in the series over a year's time.

Since then, my articles have become a part of the online collection of special projects on our site [162]. They'll be there forever. I'm still contacted every couple of weeks or so by somebody wanting more information about them. I'm now writing a book about it.

It's fascinating that, thanks to the Web's interactivity, you were able to change your article in midstream because of input from people.

Right. With email and the Web, they can see the article minutes after it appears. I'll often initiate those contacts with a phone call or email, and I'll hear back from them immediately. I really like that feedback. It used to be that we would publish a story in our newspapers and kind of hold our breath, wondering what the subject thought about them. We would not hear back from them for weeks, until they wrote an angry letter to the editor. I always like to initiate contact with the main subject, even if they're the person who looks bad in the article. I like to call them the day an article appears and ask them if it's fair and accurate. That helps *me* be sure I'm as fair and as accurate as I can be.

So, rather than feeling pressured by the increased urgency and constant deadlines that the Web has fostered, you actually welcome the increase in communication.

Yes, I love that. I think there's a lot more openness and more honest reporting nowadays, where reporters are willing to run parts of their article by experts or insiders, to make sure that they're accurate and fair, before publishing the final version.

What do you find most frustrating about the Net?

The main problem is too much information—but that's most frustrating when other people do my research for me. I also have a ten-second rule; some people say I'm being overly impatient, but if a site doesn't produce a new page in ten seconds, I move somewhere else. There's no reason to sit there looking at a page loading.

Yes, when time is money and you have to produce copy quickly, I'd say a ten-second rule sounds pretty good. What do you like best about what you do?

I like doing investigative reporting, or as I sometimes call it, public service reporting. I like seeing articles that change how people hold their governments accountable to their promises. I like to write stories that are not only interesting, but interesting *and* important. The phrase I apply to my work is a cliché, but it works: To comfort the afflicted and afflict the comfortable.

I'd like you to look forward now. How do you think researching/reporting might change over the next few years, and how do you expect it to impact what you do?

I expect to see more specialization. As software and Web resources expand exponentially, fewer people will be able to keep up with everything. We'll need more help from computer experts and Web research experts. Reporters and editors will work closer with computer specialists, and we will also put a lot more of the information we gather on the Web.

I think there will be more information online. Everyone will be able to self-publish, so newspapers and magazines will have to keep up with the best ways to present information online, not just slap-dash the article out there, but link it and expand to other sources of information online. I think interactive possibilities are greater online. TV and newspapers and magazines will come closer together and do more cooperative ventures. We'll do a lot more video. And, of course, all of it will be catalogued and saved forever on the Web for future reference.

Super Searcher Power Tips

➤ Use a team approach to investigative reporting. The technology moves so fast that it's impossible for most reporters to keep up with it, so call on specialists in computer-assisted reporting, news research, reporting, writing, and editing.

➤ Avoid the metasearch engine overload. I find that Google, Yahoo!, and Northern Light work just fine without having to search through ten or fifteen different search engines. If I need to find something very small and specific, I would use HotBot.

➤ I'll find online sources through Deja.com, Liszt, or MEDLINE. They're very valid modes for finding experts, especially in science, for finding anecdotes, and for finding people that I can call and talk to.

➤ If I'm using information I've gotten from somebody by email, I always call to verify who I'm talking to.

➤ I try to cast a wide net, and I start early with a chronology and a telephone list. I'm always looking for roadmap sources, experts who can steer me in the right direction.

➤ I have a ten-second rule. If a site doesn't produce a new page in ten seconds, I move somewhere else.

Patricia Neering

Business News Researcher for *Money* and *Fortune*

Patricia Neering is Senior Research Librarian, Business Information Group, at the Time, Inc. Research Center in New York. As coordinator of editorial research for *Money* magazine, she often consults with editors on how the research center can add value to the editorial content. She also provides research for *Fortune* magazine and the non-editorial side of the company.

patricia_neering@time-inc.com
www.timeinc.com

Tell me a bit about your background and how you came to Time, Inc.

I graduated from the University of Michigan School of Library Science in 1973. My first job was not as a librarian. I worked for a company on Wall Street tracking and forecasting the stock market using computers. For health reasons, I moved to the Virgin Islands and worked as a public school librarian from 1974 until 1983. I was then ready for a change, so I came back to New York City and got a job researching for a business television program called Business Times, which broadcast on ESPN and NPR. I stayed there until the company went out of business in 1985. The company strategy was that executives needed business news very early in the morning and did not have time to read most newspapers or magazines, so they would get their business information in a capsule before they went to work. They were ahead of the glut of business news now available. That was the first time, in 1983, that I used Lexis-Nexis [106, see Appendix], which we needed for full-text publications. Then, in September of 1985, I began working at Time, Inc. in New York.

Which publications does your research support?

When I first started, I worked for all the magazines—*People, Money, Fortune, Time, Life,* and *Sports Illustrated* [175]. There was a dedicated Nexis terminal and two other computers that we could use. This was the first time I used Dialog [44]. Computer searching was not always our first resort in doing research. At that time we did a lot of fact-checking in books and often did period-ical searches by hand using *Reader's Guide*. Lany McDonald was hired as director of the research center in 1993. She restructured the department, dividing it into three groups: News Research, which worked for *Time* magazine; Business Research, which served the financial titles and the corporate side of the company; and the Central Staff, which continues to serve all users of other departments. Around 1994, I joined the specialized section of the research center, which became known as the Business Information Group, and became a researcher for *Fortune* and *Money* magazines and for the non-editorial side of the company.

How many researchers in your group do news research for the reporters, and how did you make the transition to using the Internet?

There are nine of us altogether, although some people are part-time. We also have a manager who, among many other duties, controls the query flow and steps in with advice or research depending on the situation.

We did not use the Internet until Lany came. In the beginning, it was so exotic. I was excited about it because it seemed almost like we were reaching out into space to connect to something that seemed more real than an electronic online database.

Maybe the term "cyberspace" isn't so far-fetched. How did you become comfortable as we moved into a Web world? Did you do a lot of reading or go to seminars? Did you just do it on your own?

A combination of all of that. I remember going to Internet conferences where I'd listen to people and take lots of notes, but I didn't really have a firm concept of exactly what it was all about. I had a friend who worked in our group. He wasn't a librarian, but he had a computer in his home and he was on the Internet all the time. So, we talked about it a lot. I think he really dispelled a lot of the myths around it and made it seem like something I could do. It's funny now to think how mystical I felt it was—I had spent most of my life doing online searching, and yet I felt this might be beyond me.

What kinds of information searching do you now do to support the work at Time, Inc.? What's a typical project?

People often call because they're writing an article about a company and they need a periodical search for major profiles, from everything that is out there in the last five years. They might also want the most recent analysts' reports. If they don't know the industry very well, they might want an analysis of the industry.

Would you use the traditional online services for those sorts of requests? Or are you getting more, now, on the Net?

I would always use the traditional online databases for searches like that, but if they also want the financial filings, I will use SEC EDGAR [52]. We have a subscription to Premium EDGAR Online that we have made available through our intranet. It's easier to search and looks nicer when you print it out, but it is fee-based. It's like another site, FreeEDGAR [71], which I use all the time. Some people prefer 10-K Wizard [1]. You really have to try them to see which one works best for you. If you want analyst reports from the Internet, you can subscribe to Multex.com [126] or Investext [98], both of which are also available through Dow Jones Interactive [48], depending on what options you subscribe to. Nexis also has Investext.

What other Web resources do you use that you wouldn't have accessed before?

The Industry Standard [90]—I love that publication. You can use it for so many queries. Almost everything is Internet-related in some way. I use the *San Jose Mercury News* [161] Web site for articles and reports on Silicon Valley and Internet millionaires. They have great reports and demographics on Silicon Valley and venture capital companies in a special section on their Web site, called SiliconValley.com [163]. I also like TheStreet.com [173]. You have to pay for it, but it's very useful to see what they think about a company. They do good tutorials on topics like equity options. If I have a term that I do not understand and need basic information before I begin a traditional online search, I try the site; often, I have been pleasantly surprised. Even when the search concept is rather complex, I find helpful articles. I also like *Red Herring* [155], for information about start-up tech companies and their investors, and *Business 2.0* [28] and *Fast Company* [62], both of which have free articles about new companies and the way business is conducted in the new economy.

What do you continue to use the traditional services for?

I always use Nexis and Dow Jones Interactive, but *how* I use them depends on what the client wants. If they need in-depth coverage, I search All News on Nexis as far back as the query demands; then I supplement that with a similar search in *The Wall Street Journal, Barron's,* and *Smart Money* on Dow Jones Interactive. We don't use Dialog that much anymore, because we've negotiated better contracts with our other vendors.

The ability to do cross-file searches—all those full-text newspapers in Nexis, for instance—must be attractive, as opposed to hopping around to different sites.

It is; it saves us time and money. Sometimes, if I want a regional publication, like *The Miami Herald,* I'll search that on Dialog. If I think the story or the company is particular to Florida, I'll go to Dialog and search that one file to see what the local coverage is, just to make sure I've picked up everything. Some stories are more investigative in nature, and those are the ones I really love to work on—those are the searches where I double-check my results. Even when the same publications are covered in various online databases, each database does not always store the same articles—any one of them might miss really important articles. It's a buffer, in a way, just to make sure that we're really getting the best, but it's a time-consuming way of searching.

Can you tell me about your favorite investigative project?

I have many favorites. And it's only a recent phenomenon that librarians here are given credit for the stories they work on. I got two research credits this year. I have a fondness for the writers of those stories because of the close working relationships we developed.

One was a *Fortune* cover story called "Corporate America's Dirty Secret: Addicted to Sex." I worked on it for more than ten months. I did a lot of legal research. I think it started around the time of the congressional hearings on Monica Lewinsky, so I didn't think it was unusual that they would look for sexual addiction in executives. First, I did just general searching to see if I could find any executives who were talking about sex addiction, or any legal cases or examples. It was really difficult. I found some people, but they always seemed to work for companies that nobody had ever heard of, or else they were cases in the past that were mentioned in most articles of length. I was trying to find *new* cases.

The people at the EEOC (Equal Employment Opportunity Commission) [187] were most helpful. I spoke to a librarian in their office in Washington and she recommended certain BNA (Bureau of National Affairs) [27] newsletters on Nexis. Also, some of the spokespeople in various offices of the EEOC were helpful to talk to about big cases within their districts.

We often had to use WDS, the Washington Document Service [198], which was not an electronic service. If we did online research and could identify a case, we could call them and they would send somebody to the court to copy the file for us.

This is not something you could have gotten on the Net or in another electronic form?

I think it would have been difficult, because there were cases coming in from all over the country. Some were quite a few years ago and involved a history of filings and counter-filings. The various offices of the EEOC would send press releases, some of which were available on their Web site, but I believe the files for the cases that they investigate are not open to the public. The cases for which we had access to the documents had been filed in civil courts. The situation may change, now that Washington Document Service has been acquired by ChoicePoint [31].

So, here's an illustration that the human element is still a critical piece of your research effort.

Yes, exactly. Since I developed a rapport with the people at the EEOC, I became the contact person. I think that's the reason why

I got credit for it, because it was just the writer and me, until a reporter was assigned to the story. I may work with the writer all during a story, however long it takes to develop. I'm not really sure where the lines are drawn between what I do and what a reporter/research associate assigned to a story does. In these kinds of stories, some writers give me a lot of leeway in research-ing the story, so I can follow any leads that look good. Later, they'll get back to me as, perhaps, a contact or an angle pans out for them. We're a team of investigators collaborating, using the tools and techniques each of us knows best.

What kinds of Internet research do these reporters do? Do they typically do some, and then turn the harder searching over to you?

We're never sure how it's going to work. On our intranet we've given them access to Dow Jones Interactive and Lexis-Nexis Universe [107], so they can search those databases themselves. If they're too busy, or maybe they need more training, we might end up doing the searches anyway. Some of them use the Internet. They have all different levels of proficiency. Sometimes people even call us for telephone numbers, which we know they can find themselves. Some people seem to feel very comfortable and we don't hear from them a lot. Sometimes we wonder if they're still at the magazine!

Let's talk about the issue of data integrity and authority on the Internet. How do you deal with it and advise others to deal with it?

Some people feel comfortable with material when they're not really sure what the source is, but I don't feel comfortable with that at all. If I don't know who or what the source is, I don't trust it and I won't use it. If it's material that I think should have a date on it and there's no date, I don't use it. I will check for further informa-tion, and I'll contact the people responsible for a Web site. I tend to use sites and sources that I'm familiar with, or where I know I can trust the authority of the organization behind them. I almost always know—either through research I've done on an online database, or just on my own—where I want to go for the answer on the Internet. Once in a while I just have to throw something out there and see what comes up. But I rarely do that anymore.

I frequently use the professional online services first, unless I already know an association or organization, in which case I'll go directly to the Internet. Articles will often mention associations or other key pieces of information that I can use. Last year, I worked on a story for *Fortune* called "Lies, Damn Lies, and Managed Earnings." It was about corporations "cooking the books." I did an online search that turned up the Stanford Securities Class Action Clearinghouse [169], a development of the Robert Crown Law Library, Stanford University School of Law. It houses securities fraud class action legal documents, including summaries of complaints in which one can search alphabetically or by date to see if a company might be identified with alleged mismanagement of earnings.

The article also mentioned a law firm that had a Web site that was a depository for legal documents for companies that have had class action lawsuits filed against them, including current and prominent cases involving financial mismanagement. There was also a study entitled "Fraudulent Financial Reporting: 1987-1997; An Analysis of U.S. Public Companies" that was commissioned by the Committee of Sponsoring Organizations of the Treadway Commission. I found out about this from an article obtained from a traditional database. Then, by searching on the Internet, I found the American Institute of Certified Public Accountants [11] Web site, which mentioned how to order copies of the study.

So, I often use online databases to zero in on where to go on the Internet. I don't think that throwing a search term out on a search engine is the most efficient way to search.

Let's talk about search engines a bit. How do you use them and which ones do you find best for your purposes?

I almost always use Yahoo! [206]. I feel that it takes me where I want to go so much faster. At a recent IRE (Investigative Reporters and Editors) [99] conference, Margot Williams recommended Google [80]. So now I use a combination of Yahoo! and Google; I really don't use anything else. In fact, my bookmarks are now so out of hand that I don't even look at them anymore. I use Yahoo! or Google to go places that I used to bookmark. I have a good memory, so I might know where I want to be, but I just don't remember the URL for it.

What do you find most frustrating about the Net?

I'm frustrated by how long everything takes. I can't always tell whether it's the Net or the intranet, since we're all linked on a network. But, whether it's an internal or external slowdown, I find it irritating.

I find our job challenging. There are so many places to go for information—that's good, but it's hard to choose the best resource. For instance, we have subscriptions to AutoTrack [20] and ChoicePoint. Now, if you can't find somebody's phone number, you can always use the public records databases.

With information exploding onto the Net, what is out there that you feel is just remarkable, that you've never had access to before? And how has it changed your searching methods?

It's one thing to read in an article that somebody has published a study and to think that you could call these people and maybe they'd send you a copy of the study. On the Internet, you can go to the source of the study—whether an association or a professor's Web site at a university. You can print out the published version of the study. You don't have to wait anymore to see whether people will or will not send it to you. It's there and it's so fast. And you can give it to someone immediately.

We used to have access to Jupiter [101] and Forrester Research [69] reports. We don't currently, but you can still register as a guest and sometimes get a portion of a study for free. Sometimes that free part is all you need. I find that the paid Internet sites usually make a portion available free, and that makes research so much easier. Another one is Hoover's [85]. We used to get the print directory, but I think the Web-based product is better. You can get quite a bit for free at the site; then if you want more, you can pay.

You talked about the problem of information being available in so many different places. What are your guidelines on where to access it? Is cost the driving factor? Do the search capabilities make a difference?

All those things are factors. Sometimes it's cost. We don't use Dialog often because of their way of accounting for online costs. Sometimes speed determines the source. We have access to ProQuest [151] on the Web. It's an easy way to get full-text images of articles as they appear in magazines, with charts and photographs. But it can be a slow process. If I have to do lengthy in-depth research, I will always use a traditional online database.

It also depends on how many queries I have to deal with. If I have a lot, I try to use my time wisely, balancing the need for speed with the knowledge of which source quickly provides the best information.

I don't usually have trouble strategizing a search—if it has too many parameters, a professional database might not be the best place to find the answer. A telephone call to an expert might simplify the query. We stack queries and use the Modify option in Nexis, and then use Focus as a cost-saving strategy, stringing all our searches together throughout the day. We have both classic Nexis and Lexis-Nexis Universe. Which one we use depends on what we need. I like Universe because I think it's faster for quick, easy searches. I like the downloading feature; I can email the download to somebody, complete with page breaks and highlighted search words. We record searches, for a number of reasons, so it can be time-consuming when we log searches to disk and have to put the page breaks in and bold the search terms ourselves. I might be searching for hours, and the cleanup can be intensive. Universe does this automatically for me.

Universe doesn't pick up everything, though, that we get in regular Nexis. It has a subset of information. So, if I'm worried that I might miss something important, I don't use it. If it's a quick and dirty search, I do.

What about your use of Dow Jones?

I like Dow Jones Interactive; they did a great job with the product, including charts and tables. For some reason I've been able to find articles from, let's say *The New York Times*, on Dow Jones Interactive that I could not locate on Nexis no matter how many times I tried. I start suspecting that I've gotten the wrong information from the writer; then I do the same search on Dow Jones Interactive just to make sure, and the article turns up.

Isn't that a case where you might go to *The New York Times'* own site?

I might do that to see if the article actually appeared in *The New York Times* and to get the date, but not to access the article. If it's a fee-based site, I'd rather do the search on Nexis because I'm usually looking for a wider range of coverage than just one article from a specific journal. If I'm looking for an article and the site is free, I'll definitely access it on the Web site.

You never know why an article turns up in one database as opposed to another one. You don't know if it's because it appeared in an edition that wasn't indexed for the online database. On Dow Jones Interactive, you can choose to use the old Dow Jones codes and dot commands. I find that using the dot commands makes your searching much more precise.

So traditional searching skills are still an important part of the research toolkit, combined with new techniques for using Web resources.

Yes, searching is improved by experience in both; skills transfer from one to the other. And traditional searching is easier for someone who has made it a career! I don't think we could do our work without the traditional databases. I know it would be much more difficult. I just don't think we could identify all the sources that we need for a complex story without the traditional online services.

As the traditional services have moved over to the Web, do you feel that they have lost some of their strengths and capabilities?

I don't think the search capabilities are as good right now. I haven't quite figured out how to stack searches on Universe, for example. I think that Nexis will improve Universe, just like they worked to improve traditional Nexis, and when it comes up to the standard we're used to, more of us will migrate over to it.

Unless things change drastically for the better, we'll still need to have dial-up as backup, in case the Net crashes. Sometimes we can't get into Dow Jones Interactive on the Web, but we can dial out and pick it up through local communications.

We have Bloomberg [25], and even the Bloomberg terminal is interactive. For example, if you are on the description page for a company on the Bloomberg terminal, you can click on the URL and go to the company's Web site and then return to the typical Bloomberg screen. I love Bloomberg. It makes things a lot easier. If you just want to look at news on a company, you can go there; you don't have to search Nexis or Dow Jones. Or you can go to the company Web site and look at their press releases. If a particular service is down, there's always another way to find the answer now, which wasn't true years ago.

How do you stay updated in your field? What resources do you use to help you stay on top of search services, Internet developments, and so on?

I always look at *Searcher* [237] and periodicals like *Internet World* [234] and *Yahoo! Internet Life* [243], which we get at work. But I rely more on people. Everybody sends email to each other; people talk on library mailing lists, and send email to people in the research center, about things that they think are interesting. People within my own section talk to each other. Margot Williams from *The Washington Post* often tells me about things that she knows about. I get a newsletter and email from IRE, and I get tips there as well.

I've also been going to the IRE conferences. When I go to IRE, I feel that I'm keeping on top of things, and the programming is relevant. What I find most challenging now is working on investigative pieces, and IRE has subject-related panels for people who are investigating the military, or toxic issues, or managed care, or the prison system. Each panel provides the background for investigating a certain issue.

Speaking of search tips—is there anything that you find particularly useful, or that has gotten you through a really tough search situation?

I don't really think of them as tips, maybe more as instinct. While I'm searching, or even when I'm formatting search results, something on a page will hit me; I'll print that one page, and maybe I'll end up with twenty or thirty of those at the end. These twenty or thirty bits of information really are the sources I concentrate on, either through telephone calls, or looking for Internet sites when I get done with the traditional search. You have to be really alert, I think, when you're doing your searches. We all learn system tricks like, on Nexis, using "at least" and "word count greater than" and putting search words in the headline and maybe searching major papers—but to me, that's just formula searching and doesn't require thinking; we could do that in our sleep.

Don't discount serendipity. Sometimes you print something and you don't realize how important it is at the time, but it becomes the cornerstone of your search when you focus on it later; within the articles are hints or clues to pick up the trail. That clue may be a person or organization to contact, a research report to obtain, or a new search based on information obtained in the first run.

You mentioned earlier how important your intranet is for you. How do you decide what to put on it, and who controls that?

The research center maintains a Web site that sits on the corporate intranet. Our Web site is the main information resource for the company. Among other resources, all the research librarians who aren't managers have a favorite subject that they maintain. We find a new site every week to add to our favorites. Another librarian and I maintain the business favorites. She and I have different philosophies about what we want to post. She likes megasites; I like something that I've used in answering queries. If I have looked for a certain statistic and I know where to go to find it and I know it's official, that's something I want on our site.

It's good to have people with differing perspectives working on an intranet. I find that I often use sites that I wouldn't have posted myself; the subject area becomes more comprehensive in scope.

How do reporters and researchers share information that they've found or that is locked in their heads? Is there any mechanism for helping each other do data dumps? You don't want to keep reinventing the same research for background material.

Sometimes they put it in a shared network folder that any of us can access. A lot of that is done through the Time Magazine Group. While the story is in progress, the researchers share information on those networked folders. Sometimes my colleagues at *Time* call when they are dealing with more in-depth business stories and ask my advice about research strategies.

All of us in the Research Center work together as a team, even though we're separated into different sections. But each magazine operates as its own company; there's competitiveness there. Our work is confidential, we don't talk about stories on the elevator. We have to be circumspect about what we do.

I know that newspapers have been affected by the increased urgency that the Internet has fostered. Many of them are updating on their Web sites much more frequently than in print. Have you encountered that same compression of deadlines? Is that affecting your research?

Sure. They'll tell us right away, "I need this and I need it ASAP." They have to tell us with every query how soon they need it. Sometimes for a daily Web column they tell us, "I need it in half an hour." They're also on TV a lot. They do a lot in collaboration with CNN [34]. Not only CNN, but certain writers get asked to appear on various television shows, and for that they usually need information immediately.

We deal with all different kinds of deadlines. The same people who are writing for the Web-based product often write articles for the magazines. *Time* magazine often needs their information faster than, say, *Fortune*, because *Time* is a weekly publication.

That must put pressure on your decisions about where to research. "Where can I get it fastest?" probably supercedes "Where can I get it better?"

Yes, we constantly have to prioritize among the queries that we have. Sometimes we can negotiate for more time. We always look for the best source within the time frame we have to work in—I don't think there's ever a question about the quality of what we do.

Looking forward, how do you think research and reporting might change over the next few years, and how do you expect it to impact what you do?

For a long time I was afraid that we'd be obsolete. I think that was everybody's fear at first—to not be needed. We were afraid, even as we gave reporters and writers access to Lexis-Nexis Universe and Dow Jones, that we were putting ourselves out of a job. If people became proficient in searching, why would they need to call us? But, more and more, it's freed us up to do what we do best—we don't get as many requests for telephone numbers or one-article searches.

Clearly, we're seeing researchers becoming more like reporters and reporters becoming more like researchers, and yet they both still need each other's strengths.

Exactly. There's so little time for anybody to concentrate on their specialty or what they think they're developing into; I think it's just going to be a collaboration. And I think everything will be Net-based.

I used to think that, at a certain point, things would settle out and we would have time to assess developments, strategize, and proceed from point A to point B. But there has been no settling down in information sources and the modes of searching them, since we started using the Internet. All we can do is remain flexible and share our knowledge of how to find things, because it seems that the more we give away in know-how, the more we gain in the quality of the research we are asked to perform.

Super Searcher Power Tips

➤ If I don't know who or what the source is, I don't trust it and I won't use it. I tend to use things that I'm familiar with or where I know I can trust the authority of the organization behind them.

➤ I often use online databases to zero in on where to go on the Internet. Articles will frequently mention associations or other key pieces of information that I can use. I don't think that throwing a search term out on a search engine is the most efficient way to search.

➤ My bookmarks are so out of hand that I don't even look at them anymore. I use Yahoo! or Google to go places that I used to bookmark.

➤ I find that the paid Internet sites usually make a portion available free, and that makes research so much easier. Sometimes that free part is all you need.

➤ I just don't think we could identify all the sources that we need for a complex story without the traditional online services.

➤ It's good to have people with differing perspectives working on an intranet. I find that I often use sites that I wouldn't have posted myself.

Margot Williams

Pulitzer Prize-Winning Research Editor

Margot Williams is research editor and Internet trainer in the newsroom of *The Washington Post*. She was a member of the investigative reporting team that won the 1999 Pulitzer Prize for Public Service. She is an author and frequent speaker on research and Internet topics.

margotwilliams@twp.com
www.washingtonpost.com

Tell me a bit about your background and how you came to *The Washington Post*.

I saw the movie *Desk Set* with Katharine Hepburn and Spencer Tracy. Katharine Hepburn was a news research librarian in a broadcast news organization library, and Spencer Tracy was a computer guy who came to automate the research there. It's a great movie. The film has inspired all of us. I knew that news research was something that I really wanted to do.

After a stint as government documents librarian at Long Island University, I got a job at Time, Inc. in 1980. At that time, the library had one PC and a red Nexis terminal in the middle of the room where we took turns searching Nexis [106, see Appendix]. That was it—search Dialog [44] on the little PC and Nexis on the dedicated terminal. Time had a huge book library and an absolutely fabulous clips library, with more than twenty research librarians.

Next, I spent two years as director of a newspaper library in Poughkeepsie, New York. The *Poughkeepsie Journal* later sent me on loan to *USA Today*. That's how I got down to Washington, and eventually I landed a position at *The Washington Post*.

Tell me about the transition from searching on a Lexis-Nexis terminal to where you are today. How did you get into Internet research?

The idea that I was going to have to learn how to use the computer made a very big impact on me. It actually came upon me one Saturday, as I was sitting at the computer and couldn't figure out what I was doing when I was trying to format a disk. So I called my predecessor's husband, which is what *she* would have done. I suddenly realized, "I really have to learn how to do this."

Learning how to search online was like learning how to do research. But the biggest adjustment was learning how to use my computer competently. From that day on, I just tried to learn more and more about computers.

For a long time, I believed that there was nothing but junk on the Internet. I got comfortable with it when I became convinced that the information was worth getting. I was a pretty early user. I started writing my Internet column for the *Post* in 1994, and I'd been on the Internet a couple of years before that, before the Web, using Gopher and other pre-Web applications. But I would spend an enormous amount of time trying to hunt down information and not come up with very much. So I blew it off. I could see there was some future to the Internet, but I couldn't imagine where it was going. Before graphical user interfaces and Web search engines, it was almost impossible to use. It was only useful when I knew what agency I needed information from; then I'd go see what they had put up on their ftp site or on their gopher.

It was rather crude in those days, wasn't it?

You had to know the provenance in order to find anything—but that's still a good way of thinking about it. You stop and say, "I need demographic information. Where do I go for that?" The answer is, you go to a census bureau, or the demographics office of your local government, or somebody who does survey research. Now you go to those Web sites and see whether they've put the information there yet. This makes more sense than doing a search on Dogpile [48] for how many people live in northwest Washington, DC.

So, it's important to think about where the information is likely to be available, rather than jumping to do a general search engine search.

Yes—think about where it's always been available in the physical, real world. Traditional research practice has always been to go to the right place. The Internet can distract you with all the information that you find in the *wrong* places. But the best way, the most economical way, to search is to know either what *kind* of place you want, or how to *find* the best place to look for it. This is why I'm so adamant about using subject sites and not just going out into cyberspace on a whim. Metasearch engines like Dogpile do have their place, though—sometimes they can be really good.

When would you use a metasearch engine?

I use a metasearch engine when I'm looking for a needle in a haystack. Of course, the information has to be out there someplace in order for you to find it. If it's something really difficult or obscure, using a metasearch engine gives you a better chance of finding it, even if it's in a weird place, and then maybe finding related information.

What frustrates me is putting a name into a metasearch engine, and getting all these hits to someone's entire family genealogy. But if you have an unusual or unique topic, a metasearch is an incredible way to try to find somebody, somewhere—anywhere—who knows something about it.

The Net has certainly extended our reach. When would you still use a traditional online service for research?

I will use an online search service when I want to search across a whole body of work—for example, for legal information. The Internet is getting better and better as far as courts putting up cases is concerned, but if you go onto Lexis [106] looking for opinions, you know that you're getting just about everything. Also, the documentation tells you exactly what's available. If you're looking for an opinion and it was prior to when the cite went up on Lexis, you know it. I'm not a great legal researcher, but to the extent that I have to do legal research, I go to a traditional service. They've made so many search enhancements, too.

On the other hand, the Web is getting much better. The more government agencies and courts put up their opinions, the better it gets. But you still can't search *across* files and sources, and we do a lot of that here. Many newspapers now have their archives on the Web, but we mostly need to search across a whole bunch of newspapers. We can't really do that on the free Web. If you know specifically what date a story appeared within the past few days, and that it was in a Seattle newspaper, you can go to the Seattle papers on the Web and see what they have for the past week—and maybe get some of the photos.

Web sites are good for today's paper and maybe the past couple of weeks. I would go to the Web first, now, for that. However, when I'm searching on anything further back in time—Nexis goes back to the 1970s—I'm not going to find that on the Web.

So, the aggregation that the traditional services do is still an extremely valuable function.

Yes, the aggregation and the access to backfiles as well. For example, Thomas [174] only goes back to the early '90s for the full text of bills and laws. But Nexis has everything. And not just Nexis; some of the other online services have big backfiles of hearings and legislation and bills, in full text.

You mentioned the search enhancements that you can take advantage of with Lexis. What about the search capabilities on a traditional service versus a search engine on the Net? Does it influence your decision to know that you can do a much more targeted and precise search on Nexis or Dialog than you can on the Web?

Yes, sure. Even though we're now accustomed to relevancy searching on the Web—which is what everything is—I would never turn on the relevance-ranking in Dialog or when searching our own in-house database. We had the option of setting the in-house database to relevance ranking as the default, and no one wanted it. You want the bylines that you particularly have chosen, or you've determined which terms you want to be important. You want to decide what proximity you want those words to have relative to each other. Or you want to see the words come up in context. You want to determine the date of publication. And you always want to see things in reverse chronological order.

But that's not the way the Web works. Granted, we're not looking at eight hundred million pages when we're looking in newspaper archives. The traditional information retrieval systems are much more precise, and they're a known quantity. Once you've learned how they work, you can go back to them over and over again.

Now we say, "This search engine, AltaVista [7], has a different search protocol than Go.com [79] and MetaCrawler [120]. How can you learn all of them?" But in the past, that's exactly what we did. We were adept on several services, because every one had different search protocols. We learned different protocols for Dialog and Dow Jones [48] and Nexis and all the other systems. Each one had a different way to do it, but they were all based on Boolean logic. If you knew how to work with Boolean, you could go from one to the other. The commands might be a bit different, but you knew what you were putting in and the kind of information you would get out.

It doesn't really work that way on the Web. There are all kinds of issues. Some sites may appear at the top of your search results because a company paid for the listing. Some sites are blocked out because of registration screens or other reasons. So the scope of coverage is undefined at this point—you really don't know what you're looking at. You don't know how deeply a site is indexed. You don't know what period of time is covered.

You talked about using Nexis because you can search across newspapers. Do you use other services, such as Dow Jones or Dialog?

Yes. Dow Jones and Lexis-Nexis are very similar except for the legal materials in Lexis and the business information in Dow Jones, and the differences in which newspapers and wire services are available on each. Dow Jones publications are on Dow Jones, and the backfile of *The New York Times* and various foreign papers are on Nexis. Dialog has the Knight-Ridder papers, which aren't on either of the others. So, it's still a three-way race.

You really need all three to cover all the bases?

Yes. You have to have them all or else you can't cover a beat. You don't want to say, "Well, I can do the search for you, but I can't get you *The Wall Street Journal*." That's ridiculous. You also don't want to say, "I can't get you *The New York Times*," or "You can't see *The Miami Herald*," or the smaller newspapers where there's a lot of valuable information.

But newspapers aren't everything we search. For example, there are several places to go for Dun & Bradstreet [50]. It's available in Lexis-Nexis now, but different reports are available on Dialog.

When you get an information request or an article assignment and you're working with a

reporter, do you have a general method that you have worked out? How do you decide where to begin?

I've been thinking a lot about that; I might have said I did a lot by instinct. But it's more like habit, or maybe just experience—more than twenty years of answering reporters' questions. My method depends on what kind of a question it is. To some extent, the time limitations will determine where I look. But economics are important too. It might be worth my time to spend more money. But things change. Using Nexis used to be expensive. But when we converted to flat-fee pricing, then Nexis wasn't the most expensive resource. A good researcher must be flexible. We need intellectual flexibility, and flexibility in managing the information sources that are available. We need to be able to weigh the pros and cons of what to do and where to go—and to make those decisions quickly.

Another issue is the availability of customer service. That's another reason to stay with the traditional services, because there are help lines and people to help you. You can talk to people on the phone at Nexis and Dow Jones. If you need something in the middle of the night, somebody will be there to help you—and you get very good help. It's not like calling software companies and waiting on hold for hours.

If you're a wise customer, you can get all kinds of resources from the companies you deal with. That is another good reason to use traditional sources—they have their users in mind. Internet sites don't have users in mind. Quite frequently, you don't even know who you're dealing with; there's no phone number to call and no way to get in touch with somebody, except maybe email to a Webmaster.

Have you found that to be a problem?

Yes. I don't use a site if I don't know who put the information there and I can't get in touch with them. In the book I did with

Nora Paul, *Great Scouts!* [231], we didn't recommend any sites where you couldn't find a real person to call.

How do you deal with verification of sources? What types of sources and how many are required to use a piece of information? Has the Internet complicated this, or made it easier?

The researchers at *Time* labeled sources as "red-check" or "black-check." A red-check source is something that came from an information source itself. For example, the spelling of someone's name in *Who's Who* as they submitted it. Or if someone's the author of a book, you get the title page with the name.

The other kind of source is like what you see in the newspaper. Newspaper writing is what Philip Graham called a "first rough draft of a history." You try to get it as right as you can the first day. If you don't have enough information, or the right information, maybe you have to go back the next day and go deeper, or go over the story. You know that mistakes turn up in newspapers a lot. They correct them, hopefully. But one article from one newspaper that mentions somebody's name is not a good enough source, by itself, to repeat in print.

Information from the Web can be used as background, or as a resource for finding people and getting better information straight from a person's mouth. But copying directly from somebody's Web site is definitely not recommended. You can find out who owns a Web site by checking who registered the domain name. You can go into the Whois database at Network Solutions [203] and put in the domain name, such as WashingtonPost.com [199]. You get the name of the person who registered the site, along with a phone number and address, and possibly some technical person to get in touch with. At least you get a clue about where you can call to find out more. If somebody just has some Web server space on AOL [10], you can't really get to them. AOL and Internet service providers won't give out the names of their customers. So, if somebody doesn't indicate on their Web page who they are, it can take quite a bit of digging. If you are on a deadline, you would not go to all that effort to try to confirm the information that appears on a Web site.

When you're using a traditional information source, you know where the information came from. Of course, errors turn up there, too, but you know that, when you're searching *The Miami Herald*, you're getting a story that was in *The Miami Herald*, and you can cite it as such. Things are changing, but I still would use Web sites differently than traditional information sources.

What can you get access to on the Net that you couldn't get before?

I think the thing that's made the greatest impact on my job is that you can get just about any newspaper in the world now. Today's paper. Practically every newspaper is online. Reporters used to say to us, "I need to see today's *Louisville Courier*," and then we'd have to call some guy and beg him to fax us the paper that day. It really hit us during the Whitewater investigation, when we were calling Arkansas and asking them to fax us that day's paper—the whole paper! Finally we worked out a paying arrangement with them. Librarians have always been able to search the archives, but the reporters always wanted today's paper, not last week's. We'd have to beg, borrow, and do whatever we could to get it. It made all the news librarians closer, because we got to talk to everybody all the time. We really had to help each other out because we have, for the most part, very small libraries.

Another important resource we now have is public records. For example, the candidates in many states and in the federal government now have to file their campaign finance records in electronic form. Government agencies have put them up and made them available during the political campaigns. Any of the presidential candidates who are getting federal matching funds have to file their campaign contribution reports electronically on the FEC (Federal Election Commission) [189] Web site, and they're up the same day. That's a huge difference from the days of searching the FEC electronic bulletin board. It's only for presidential campaigns, so far, but you can see where it's moving. You can get New Jersey campaign finance contributions going back to the 1980s. That's been a huge public service.

Another thing that's come up recently—it's not altogether there yet—is the IRS form 990 [128] from charitable organizations. If you're giving to a charity, you might want to know something about that charity, like how much money they have and how much they spend on themselves, as well as how much they actually give to the people that you think you're giving to. Now those IRS filings are being made available on the Web. In the past, you had to go to the IRS office here in Washington, DC, to look at them. Or you had to go to the office of the institution, and they were required to show them to you. But, they could determine *when* you could come to see them and *what* they would show you. Now, it's all going to be up on the Internet, which is just the way it should be.

There's been some controversy about listing the sex offenders in an area online. Many jurisdictions have that information on the Web. People who are on parole are sometimes listed, depending on where they live. There's a lot of information that the public is demanding to be put up on the Web, and the agencies are seeing it as their responsibility to make it available to citizens. For me as a researcher, that's a big plus. Corporation records and such are now online, so you can see who owns that company in Maryland.

It's a huge boon that you can find information from all over the world instantaneously. Government documents, like the Uniform Crime Reports from the FBI [184], are being published right to the Web; we no longer have to wait for them to be delivered to depository libraries. It's even better because you sometimes get the actual data that the agency used to publish in print. You can drop it into a program like Excel [253] or database software like Access [252], and look at it yourself, and look at it in different ways. You're not dependent on the agency to tell you what the data mean. That's where the computer-assisted reporting field is going. We can take the data the government has collected, and manipulate and analyze it, and come to our own conclusions rather than just what they tell us at the press conference.

Let's talk about the different kinds of information searching that researchers and reporters do.

I feel that we're better at casting the big net. As researchers we're so adept at using the search tools that we can get through a huge amount of information more quickly and precisely and pull out relevant items. We can be more precise in retrieval. I think that reporters may get frustrated with the volume of information.

Reporters tackle different kinds of information tasks. One task is coming up with a story idea. That's the broadest question of all. We can't really come up with a story idea for a reporter. They have to get an idea. In order to get an idea, they want to see all kinds of information that may or may not be related. They need to see what other people have been doing, but they don't want to copy what others have been doing. That's often the hardest part for us, because we don't know exactly what they're looking for. The reporters need to be enabled to do more of that on their own; desktop access to the Internet and commercial online services has helped them do more. And now, training reporters to find information on the Web and in the online archives is part of our jobs, too.

Once they have an idea, another task is to gather all of the information that might be pertinent to the idea. I have the wonderful luxury of being in a place where reporters work on big projects, so they have more time. Even when they're on a shorter-term project, they try to get a lot of background and information from many sources. So, first there's the story-idea type of question, and then there's the story backgrounder, where we pull together all kinds of information and the reporter goes through it to decide what might be relevant.

Then there's the task of looking for people, looking for sources. That's where a kind of convergence is occurring, because that's what reporters do; they look for people to talk to.

Reporters still tend to do the shoe-leather interviewing and reporting, but now we're helping them find people to talk to, much more than we had in the past. We have so many more tools to do it online. In the past, what did we have? We had a crisscross directory for finding names and addresses when we had the phone numbers. We could call directory assistance. We could look in the *Encyclopedia of Associations* [54] or the other places we'd look to find an expert.

Reporters tended to use the same experts over and over, just because they'd spoken to them before. Now, with the Internet, we can seek out people whom we don't know. We can find people who are experts in a professional field, or who have actually suffered from a disease, or hobbyists who are experts in some way. The Internet is an incredible way to get in touch with people. We have to be mindful of the fact that these are just the people who are *on* the Internet. But it's not like a few years ago when we only got young white men if we looked for sources on the Internet. Now it's a lot more diverse.

Despite some convergence, though, don't reporters and researchers each have special skills? Isn't it best to work as a team that utilizes everyone's strengths?

Right. Reporters are known for being great reporters. Some are known for being great writers. For the most part, even though we researchers do know how to write, writing for the newspaper is usually off our radar. But when I work as a researcher on a team with reporters and editors, I have to write up what I've come up with, not just dump a pile of papers on the reporter's desk. We used to just do the online searches and give the stack of paper to the reporter.

So, they expect you to do some processing and information filtering for them.

Definitely. I believe that they always wanted us to do that, but there was a lack of communication; they didn't really press us. In order to filter, however, we needed to have done a reference interview, to know exactly what kind of information they were looking for. So, it's a two-way street; we need to be better interviewers.

On the other hand, reporters have always wanted to be able to get online and have access to the same resources we do, so that they too can use serendipity in the way that we frequently do. My idea of a serendipitous find may be different from the reporter's. Sometimes we are lucky and we come up with something really interesting that they didn't ask us for. However, if they know how to use the tools, they're more likely to get an advantage out of being able to do it themselves. They can make their own connections.

Do you ever get credit for your research?

Our investigative researcher, Alice Crites, has worked on many attention-getting projects this year for which she's been credited. She has the opportunity to get credit because she's on the investigative team, doing work in-depth. They work on projects for months, and she's part of that. Alice and I worked together on "Deadly Force," a five-part series of articles that appeared at the end of 1998 and won the 1999 Pulitzer Prize for Public Service.

You must take particular pleasure in that one.

I do, because the team included two researchers, two computer-assisted reporting experts, four reporters, two editors, people who worked in graphics, and people who worked on the photography. It was a real team effort that was eight months in the making. And it turned out very well. We're very proud of our part in that. We were made to feel that we were a part of the whole process, through the prize-winning and the parties and everything else. It was a really great experience for Alice and me.

But there's a lot more for the researchers to get into at *The Washington Post*. The Metro researcher gets credit just about every day for hunting down somebody who was either the criminal or the victim, on really short deadlines. It's the same with the people in Financial and in Foreign, where we have researchers out on the desks. At this point, we're beefing it up. We have two people in National for the elections. That's a big change for us. The rest of the staff is still in the library, which is located between the main newsroom and the Investigative desk.

We have a model that a lot of other news libraries are either investigating or actually starting to adopt, which is putting the researcher right out next to the reporters and making them that much closer to the story, not just doing research for reporters from a centralized library. The desk researchers are also tasked with helping reporters and editors learn how to make better use of their computers to do research. We can just walk right over to someone who's having a problem with Dow Jones or Nexis, or with the Internet, or with our intranet, and sit with them. Each minute that we spend like that with someone is so worthwhile.

What is on the intranet at the *Post* and how do you decide what to put on it?

The Web is expanding so fast, and so much more information, particularly government information, is being collected electronically and put up on the Web. One of the main choices we have to make is whether we're going to go to the effort to put it up on our intranet, which we call The Source. We don't have a special intranet staff; it's a newsroom-wide effort, and we have a basic stake in doing it.

We have to know what people want. It's not a matter of the library telling people what they need; it's much more finding out from the reporters and editors what they would like to see. Sometimes they want the expense form, so they can fill out their expenses electronically. Or they'd like to be able to look at land records. Then we have to figure out a way to get the land records on the intranet. It's not worth putting a lot of effort into something if they don't need it, or if it's available someplace else.

That's another reason to keep up with what's happening on the Internet, so that you're not duplicating something that's easy to use someplace else. In some cases, you might want to do that anyway, but in others you wouldn't. For example, campaign finance information is available in many places on the Web right now. But, because we're so heavily into using campaign finance information and it's a major part of our reporting, we also have it in-house. We have campaign finance information for the presidential candidates, for example. We also have built campaign finance databases for the District of Columbia, Maryland, and Virginia, for our Metro reporters. We have those in-house for the reporters to use on our intranet. We have voter registration information. We didn't have to build it, but we bought it and put it in a form for the reporters or anybody in the newsroom to use. But we don't have to make our intranet another Yahoo!. We don't need to create a guide to everything on the Web. We can point people to the *other* guides on the Web.

What kinds of guides do you have on your intranet?

We've started to put up either reference-related pages, like how to find people, or beat-related pages, like how to look for court information. It's not only Internet sources, but other information, too, like what book to use, the address of the courthouse, the name of the clerk, and the phone number. These are really labor-intensive projects. You can't just do "my favorite list of places to go." You have to pick and choose the ones that are going to be most useful for reporters. We thought courthouse and court information would be useful, and our Supreme Court reporter helped put that together. Our financial researcher, Richard Drezen, wrote up how to look for basic company information—not for business reporters, but for other people who might have to look for companies and would not know how to do it, or would call a researcher to do it for them. The newsroom has many resources available now that we can point people to, so that they can do it themselves.

And, to a great extent, the reporters and editors would prefer to do it themselves, if they have the time.

However, sometimes things don't work right. We can't depend on a resource being available in just one place. It's important to have some kind of backup all the time. I'm still very much against throwing the books out. Even if we have the *Encyclopedia of Associations* on GaleNet [75], which is a subscription service, we have the book in the library. Sometimes GaleNet isn't working, our Internet connection is slow, or the reporter doesn't know, or can't get to a computer. The *Encyclopaedia Britannica* [53] is online now, but what if they decide that it's not going to be there anymore?

It sounds like you believe in being prepared.

In the news business, we have to be prepared. Things always happen, everything's a crisis, and something happens every day that's never happened before. But certain kinds of events also recur. We had four plane crashes, for example, in just a couple of months, including John Kennedy's plane and EgyptAir. But every time it happens, we start doing the search all over again: Where do I go to find this, and where do I go to find that? It's actually not that hard to systematize the process and try to make a pathfinder for the steps you would go through if a certain type of event happened. When a plane crashes, where would you go to find information about the plane, about the pilot, about the place where it crashed, about the company that made the plane, the record of accidents of that company or that plane, or the address of the pilot and his phone number and his family's name? These are the things we deal with when there's a plane crash. The victims of the accidents, where they come from, what their background is—things that people would like to know about the people who have died.

So, a pathfinder is a guide if you have to think quickly: Here's how to walk through this kind of research.

Some people have gone through it before. Or some people are more familiar with that type of research than others. On a newspaper, we're there seven days a week and we're there until all hours. Web news organizations are there twenty-four hours a day. We don't have to be there twenty-four hours a day, but *I* may not be there on Sunday night when a plane goes down. I know where they can get the tail number. Someone else may know something else that's important. Pathfinders would be good for where to go when there's an earthquake, a hurricane, a fire, or the mayor's arrested, or the President is shot. It's always going to be a crisis, but we could have some kind of center to go to if we prepare in advance. So that's what we're trying to do.

Our reporters now have access to many of the same resources that the researchers did originally, like Lexis-Nexis and Dow Jones and all these Web sites and CD-ROMs that we have on our intranet and on our network now. So these guides are not just for the four librarians who happen to be there that day; they're something that people can be working on along with us, or doing even when we're not involved.

How do you stay updated in your field when you have so much ground to cover?

We have eleven researchers. Everyone is constantly keeping everyone else updated on what they are interested in, or what they have found out. People subscribe to different electronic mailing lists and read different professional literature. We don't all read the same thing. The researchers meet every day at noon; we talk about what's going on in our sections and we trade information. We try to coordinate what we're doing.

We also use email to group-broadcast to other researchers and to other people that we think might be interested. We frown upon sending messages out to everybody in the newsroom about a great new site. Not everyone wants to hear about it, but one specific person might be very interested.

What lists do you subscribe to and find useful?

The Scout Report [220], including the Scout Report for Business and Economics, the Scout Report for Social Sciences, and the Scout Report for Engineering. Also ResearchBuzz [219], and the Internet TOURBUS [215]. A guy in Georgia has been doing the TOURBUS for years. It's not aimed at researchers in particular. I used to subscribe to Net-happenings [217], but there was just so much every day that I couldn't take it anymore.

I subscribe to the SLA News Librarian list, NewsLib [222]; almost all news librarians in the country subscribe to that. We help each other out and trade information. I subscribe to NICAR-L [218], the National Institute for Computer-Assisted Reporting. I'm not on CARR-L [212],Computer Assisted Research and Reporting, right now; I go in and out. Elliott Parker runs that one. IRE-L [216] is another. I'm not on that all the time, either. I'm always on NICAR and NewsLib. Some of the lists I get in digest form, but then I end up not reading them all the way through. I read *Searcher* [237], *EContent* [227], and *Online* [235] magazines.

The hardest thing for me to keep up with—and I don't think anyone is really doing a good job of it—is what's available where, online through various vendors and on the Internet, and doing comparative shopping. Sometimes, I find good articles about this in professional periodicals like *Searcher*. But it's important everyday. It's something that we should do a much better job with as consumers of information products. We use public records providers, for instance, to locate people and their phone numbers, and information about individuals and companies. There are several competing vendors. It's very hard to figure out which one is best, what's available where, and what the cost comparisons are. It's hard to find enough time to do that. Or, for example, to compare which court systems are available on all the different services and on the Web, and what years are covered, and which are abstracts and which are full text and which are docket number listings. We should be doing all this for ourselves and for our users.

If *you* have a hard time sorting through and deciding where to go for things, think about reporters.

Right. We've done a few things to help them, since reporters now have access to some of the commercial online providers. We have created resources on our intranet so they can find which newspapers are covered for which years on each of the services they search. There's also a guide to which wire services are covered and which aren't, which foreign news sources are covered, and which transcript services are covered. We made the time to do that. There are so many other resource and comparison guides that we should be doing. I think that's a very big part of our new role—we are no longer intermediaries, but rather information coaches and scouts and guides. We're responsible for turning people into wise consumers, not just saying, "Here's the password." There's a lot of work to be done in helping users make better choices about their information tools.

Looking ahead, how do you think research and reporting methods might change over the next few years? And how will it impact what you do?

I think there could be both positives and negatives. On the one hand, look at the impact that the Web has had on information distribution, the negative side being that all kinds of things can be put up there without being checked. You can post news or gossip or rumor, and make it available to the world without any kind of editorial oversight. Will we see just a bunch of unverified facts or opinions online? Advertising, opinion, news—they all start to blur. You wonder whether anybody will need people to check facts for them if the world goes beyond expecting real facts. I don't think that's really going to happen. But the volume of information that's available and the accessibility of it all will continue to have a big impact on us.

With so many small niches around the Web, it's going to be really hard to keep track for the people that need to use them.

Maybe each person who's a reporter or a professional in their narrow field will be able to keep track of their own personal group of information sources. But, if you look at it more broadly, it's going to be hard to do.

I view some of the niche or subject-oriented portals as very helpful, in the sense that they aggregate and pull together information that people need in a particular vertical area. But, I find that it's hard even to keep track of those.

I hope we'll see more niche portals, and that we will continue to benefit from the work of individual scholars, experts, and enthusiasts who have put together these areas for a subject that they're interested in, or a subject that they're teaching. Most of the best subject guides are labors of love, or something people have done as part of their job as a librarian or a professor or as a graduate student. With the increasing commercialization of the Web, I don't know if these vigorous, just-for-the-love-of-it kinds of sites are going to continue to be as well distributed as they are now.

There's a very good site that's about Right to Life—and that's the only opinion you get, a guide to all the Right to Life materials [183]. But you have to balance that out with another site that has a list of pro-choice resources. Neither of those are sites that will be commercially viable. It's still going to take people who are interested in their topics to provide this information as a service to others. Many of the best subject sites are these specialist, hobbyist, or amateur services.

With some of the portal sites, one hopes that they aren't just gathering the *most* subject information, but the *best*. And that they don't want to have just one point of view, or one commercial interest, but many points of view. I'd like to see better sites for quality, not quantity. I think librarians are the best at putting this kind of material together, because of our more objective view; that's my subjective opinion, anyway.

Maybe someday there will be a software product that will be able to analyze everything and pull it into all those different subject areas, and tell you what's the best. But I'm not holding my breath. I think it takes people and experts.

One thing about being a news researcher is that I'm not an expert on anything. I just know where to try to find experts, or places where people are experts. In a job like ours, you can be asked anything about anything. I used to feel like I was playing Trivial Pursuit all the time. I feel less like that now, either because I've gotten used to it, or because there's so much more information available that people can answer their own trivia questions. But people can still ask me anything on any day—and that is the real pleasure of the job.

Super Searcher Power Tips

➤ The Internet can distract you with all the information that you find in the *wrong* places. But the best way, the most economical way, to search is to know either what *kind* of place you want, or how to *find* the best place to look for it. This is why I'm so adamant about using subject sites and not just going out into cyberspace on a whim.

➤ If it's something really difficult or obscure, using a metasearch engine gives you a better chance of finding it, even if it's in a weird place, and then maybe finding related information.

➤ A good researcher must be flexible. We need intellectual flexibility, and flexibility in managing the information sources that are available. We need to be able to weigh the pros and cons of what to do and where to go—and to make those decisions quickly.

➤ You sometimes get the actual data online that the agency used to publish in print. You can drop it into a program like Excel or database software like Access, and look at it yourself, and look at it in different ways. You're not dependent on the agency to tell you what the data mean.

➤ We have a model that a lot of other news libraries are either investigating or actually starting to adopt, which is putting the researcher right out next to the reporters and making them that much closer to the story, not just doing research for reporters from a centralized library.

➤ We don't have to make our intranet another Yahoo!. We don't need to create a guide to everything on the Web. We can *point* people to the other guides on the Web.

Elisabeth Donovan

"Herald"ed Newspaper Research Whiz

Liz Donovan is Research Editor and Pulitzer-Prize winning news researcher for *The Miami Herald*. She is responsible for all research, training, systems/research coordination, and the newsroom intranet. She was a national desk researcher at *The Washington Post* during the Watergate years, and did special research for Woodward and Bernstein.

edonovan@herald.com
www.herald.com

I understand you have a long history of news research experience. Tell me about your background and how you came to *The Miami Herald*.

I've been in news research since 1968 when I walked into *The Washington Post* looking for a job after college. My first job was in the promotions department pasting up entries for all the prizes, including the Pulitzer Prize. I learned where the library was because I had to go and find clippings of the stories that had run in the past year. I hadn't even known newspapers had libraries, so it was a shock to see that there was a whole department of people cutting and filing stories.

After the awards season was over, I got a job in the library, and worked there about seven years. I didn't have a library degree. I had majored in political science and then gone to Washington hoping to get a job in politics, working in a congressional office or something like that. But, it turned out that I found myself the best job in the whole world, and I hadn't even known that such a job existed. I just fell into research. I was good at it from the beginning, and I knew it was what I really liked doing most of all.

And you just happened to be at *The Washington Post* during some of the most interesting times.

Some of the things that I got to do were just incredible. One example is the Pentagon Papers, which involved going through all the old clips from Vietnam with a reporter, trying to match incidents that were mentioned in the Pentagon Papers with the actual stories that ran at the time. It was a dirty job; it meant going through boxes and up ladders in a dusty storage room.

What about online library research?

Not at the *Post*. *The New York Times* Information Bank started, I think, in '67 or '68. Sometimes we'd call the researchers at the *Times'* Washington bureau and ask them to look up a story for us if we really couldn't find it any other way. I never actually saw the Information Bank in action, but my boss, Mark Hannan, who ran the library at the *Post*, had seen it demonstrated. He thought it was the worst thing he'd ever seen and said he would never have a computer in the library as long as he was there. Which actually turned out to be true, because it wasn't until he retired that the *Post* computerized. This was probably in the late '70s or early '80s, long after I'd left.

It's amazing how far we've come in a short amount of time.

In giving speeches about what I do, I've talked about the differences between research during Watergate and now. During Watergate, I had actually been asked by Carl Bernstein to become their full-time researcher. It was late summer of '72, and the *Post* was looking bad because nobody else was pursuing the story, and a lot of people thought that we were really going out on a limb. I didn't want to quit my library job, but I agreed to put in as much overtime as it took to help them with their book. And so I started clipping. And that was my job, clipping all the stories about Watergate from all the major newspapers like *The New York Times* and the *Post*, and the newsmagazines, *Time* and *Newsweek*.

Think what a different task it would be today to look for the same kind of information.

Yes, it would be! We had some things filed by subject in the *Post* clipping files, but my file was chronological, because that made the most sense to us at the time. So, we had to know what day something happened if we were going to be able to find the reference to it. I often talk about the scene in *All the President's Men* where Bob Woodward is sitting in the *Post's* library with a huge stack of *Who's Who*s and he's trying to find Kenneth Dahlberg. The Miami prosecutor's office had found a $25,000 check in the bank account of one of the burglars, signed by Kenneth Dalhberg. They didn't know who he was. In the scene, a librarian comes in and says, "We don't have a clipping file on a Kenneth Dahlberg, but I found this in the photo files." It was a picture of Dahlberg at a Minnesota political meeting in 1966 or '68, handing a check to Hubert Humphrey. For some reason, somebody in the library had chosen to file that photo under the name of this person who would probably never be mentioned again in *The Washington Post*. And the librarian in 1972 just happened to look there, in desperation, and there he was.

Woodward got on the phone and called directory assistance in Minneapolis and St. Paul, and found Kenneth Dahlberg. And Dahlberg said, "Oh, I gave that check to Maurice Stans." Stans was the Nixon reelection committee's finance chief. And that started the whole thing. That was the first connection between the burglars and the campaign committee. So, I've always been very proud of the library, and the librarian, whoever it was. Nobody remembers now which of the *Post's* librarians it was who found the photo, but the woman in the film looks like me, so people believe it was me. I just don't remember.

Now, you would probably look for the same types of information and connections, only in a different way.

Sure. We would go to phone listings on CD or Internet phone directories, put his name into Nexis [106, see Appendix] or another online news service, and we would find news stories about him, and his phone number. Something that took several hours back then can now be done in a few minutes online. Also, after I came to *The Miami Herald*, the first year that we did an anniversary of the Watergate story I went back and looked at all *The Miami Herald* stories about the break-in. There had been some great stories; the burglars were all from Miami, after all. But in Washington in 1972, we didn't get *The Miami Herald*, and there was no way to see those stories. Today, I would have been able to go to Dialog [44] or to the *Herald*'s archive on NewsLibrary [124] and look it up immediately. The depth of research that we can do now is so superior to what we had then. But they did great journalism back then, too. Sometimes I wonder how they did it.

Tell me how you made the transition to doing online research.

When I moved to Miami, I went to work for Nora Paul at *The Miami Herald*. Nora had just gotten a subscription to BRS, which offered access to *The New York Times* Information Bank online. I was still dubious about computers for news research, and the Information Bank's bibliographic database was minimally useful because it didn't give us full text of articles. But when I learned that it was a fast way to find out what stories were out there and how to search using keywords that might not have been listed in an index, I got hooked on it quickly. Within the next year, we got Nexis, which gave us access to full-text news stories. Of course, we had a very small budget, so we had to be really careful about how much we used it. As we proved how useful it was, though, we got to increase the budget.

Over the years we added resources like local real estate records. Local Florida corporate records became available on CompuServe [35]. We added Dialog and Dow Jones [49] and local court records access. I ended up managing access to the databases and wrote instructions for people to use. When the Internet came along, I began to keep lists of links, which I put on the network eventually.

Since we've had a full-fledged intranet, we've added lots of end-user subscriptions so that all reporters can search Nexis, Dialog, InfoUSA [95], and ProQuest [151], among other things. We have about thirty-five searchable databases of local government data that we've put online, including drivers' licenses, car registrations, voting records, campaign contributions, local government employees, criminal records, and workers' comp records. We recently hired a database editor to keep our in-house databases updated. We also subscribe to three different public records services.

We have fewer researchers now than we've ever had. So we rely on the reporters to do most of their own searching. My job is to try to teach them to search and to control their usage when it costs money. I have to keep the budget under control.

Do the librarians and news researchers pitch in when reporters are having trouble or need additional help?

Right. We do much less primary searching now for reporters, although there are—and always will be, I'm sure—some reporters who are uncomfortable doing it themselves. I spend increasingly more time showing people where to find things on the Internet, or suggesting where they might go to find certain types of public records, government reports, and so on. I do the more complicated searches in Nexis and Dialog for people who get hundreds of stories and don't know how to cut it down to a reasonable number.

Do you work with reporters in teams?

That's certainly an ideal. I try to go to some news meetings every week to learn what's coming up. But with our limited staff, it's not always easy to get deeply involved in projects. I'm in the newsroom, and I'm there to act as the first line for questions from reporters. We have one reference person in the library who handles the book requests, retrieves photos, and takes some online research requests. The two of us are the research staff. The library manager, Gay Nemeti, does some research too, along with a researcher in our biggest bureau. But both of them have other responsibilities in managing and enhancing our own archive. So it's hard for us to work in teams because there just aren't enough of us. We are included in some big projects, though. The best example was the vote fraud project that won a Pulitzer Prize. It was definitely a structured team project, and that was part of the reason that it was so good.

Tell me about that award-winning project.

We had an election for mayor of Miami in November '97. The then-mayor, Xavier Suarez, was beaten by Joe Carollo by a very small margin, which required a run-off election, held two weeks later. An inordinate number of absentee ballots were filed, and Suarez got the majority—mostly from the absentee votes. It looked fishy. Judy Miller, the projects editor at the time, now city editor, decided that we needed a full-fledged investigation. It started as a computer-assisted reporting (CAR) project: Dan Keating, the city desk's CAR editor (now at *The Washington Post*) got the voter registration and voting database. He ran those records against felony records, city employee records, real estate records, and social security death records databases. He came up with a list of people who appeared to be dead but who had still voted; people who worked for the city of Miami, didn't seem to live in the city, but had still voted there; addresses that seemed to house more voters than there was room for; and people who had voted despite having felony records. There were a few hundred people to look at more closely. That's when the real project started: All those people had to be backgrounded to find out if they truly were felons, or if they truly were dead, or if they truly didn't live in the city of Miami.

What a huge research project!

Yes. Judy got several departments to lend her reporters for a couple of months, and put them all on the vote fraud team. Their job was to do the reporting on these people. They had to do background checks on all of them, which meant going through some of the public records databases that we had online, like AutoTrack [20], and county databases.

My job was to train all these people in how to use online public records. Over the years, we had been training reporters to do background checks as they covered elections. So we had a group of reporters who were trained, but we had to update them on the changes in online records, as well as train those who were new at it. So we held a couple of classes for the team.

Then we needed to give them access to some databases that aren't available online, like the voting records database that Dan had obtained. I'd been talking up the idea of an intranet with searchable databases on it for a couple of years, but our systems department didn't have the capability yet. Luckily, the promised Internet server arrived just about the time we were starting to work on this project. I finally convinced our systems department to give us access, and Dan put the voter database on the intranet and set it up so the reporters could search it. He set up other databases where team members could input the information they'd found on each subject, and others could go over the records. It was a wonderful interactive computer-assisted reporting project on a lot of different levels.

Of course, the other thing that I had to do was pay for all the online research that the reporters were doing on the commercial databases. For a couple of months, we went over our budget by a factor of two. So, for the rest of the year, I had to figure out a way to keep our spending in line. Luckily, as Dan added more databases to the intranet, it reduced the need for some of our online searching.

I often had to do quick searches for the team members. They were also going out, knocking on doors, trying to find out who lived in certain houses—say, a house that had nine voters in it, but was only a two-bedroom house. They'd call me from their car or a phone booth and say, "I'm at this house. Can you tell me who owns it, or who lives here?"

It was a huge project, and I'm so thrilled that it's the one that won the Pulitzer, because it involved so many people—twenty-two of us in all—and when it came time to nominate it for awards, everyone was given credit. It was just wonderful.

Let's talk about the importance that your intranet played in this project. Can you imagine doing all that without being able to put up all that information and share it and have access to it? Wasn't the intranet really key to this project?

Before the intranet, the only way to do it would have involved gathering paper, taking lengthy notes, filing them into folders, and hoping none got lost. With the intranet, though, the reporters were actually creating a database of the information that they'd gathered. Without the intranet, they wouldn't have had access to the voting records. Voting records aren't public records in Florida—one of the few states where they aren't—so they aren't online anywhere. We would have had to rely on the one copy on one computer.

Since we couldn't get access to the database directly, we obtained it under the table, and didn't know if anyone would challenge the legality of our having it. I think we proved the value of its being available to news organizations, and recently a state attorney general opinion seems to have reversed the prevailing attitude about its availability. It was a great resource for us.

The interactivity of that entire project made it special. We would probably have had a hard time putting it all together otherwise. It was interesting to see the problems that we discovered, too, and the insights we gained from some of the data. For instance, in matching the voter list to the social security death filings, we found lots of supposedly dead people who had voted. Many of them proved to be alive, though; it turned out only one "voter" was truly dead. This led us to realize that social security death filing data are not accurate at all. Maybe it's because people have filed fraudulent claims, or there've been typos when the social security numbers were entered.

But we did find several felons who had voted, and many people who worked for the city of Miami, or were related to people who worked for the city of Miami, who actually didn't live in the city of Miami and so weren't eligible to vote there—but did anyway. We also found someone who was buying votes for ten dollars each. After several stories reporting these discrepancies, the election was overturned by a court and several people were indicted.

Many of the files that were critical to your research are not available on the public Internet, but are databases that you had to purchase, correct?

Right. In some cases, they had been acquired for previous computer-assisted projects. We are always gathering databases from the city, county, and state governments, and many of these already had been gathered and were sitting on Dan Keating's computer, but we had no way for other people to search them. In many cases you can get them from government agencies for a minimal charge, usually the cost of transferring the data. As the fraud project went on, Dan added more and more of those databases to the intranet.

So many people think, "I can get everything on the Internet." Your experience proves that some key resources are not available on the Net—or on the standard online search services such as Dialog, Lexis-Nexis, or Dow Jones.

Right. And in many other states, the information isn't available even to news organizations. One of the joys of working in Florida is that it has the most liberal sunshine laws of any state; almost everything is a matter of public record in Florida. You can get access to data that other states close off. If we'd been in New York or Georgia, for instance, we might have had much more trouble doing that project.

There's also the question of search capabilities. I can search drivers' licenses from online vendors like AutoTrack or Public Records Online [152], and I can search felon records at the Florida Department of Corrections Web site [68], but I can only search for one name at a time. I can't pull down a large chunk of data and match names from two different databases. That's another way that computer-assisted reporting contributes to a project like this. With the databases loaded locally, I can pull out large groups of records that match certain criteria. I can't do that with the online databases.

So, you use a mix of traditional online services, proprietary public records databases, and the Internet. You sift through a lot of resources, and you ask reporters to do quite a bit as well.

You're right; this is a lot of data. Part of the frustration and challenge of my job these days is guiding reporters on where to go to get the best data. For example, if they want to get a driver's license or somebody's address and phone number, we may subscribe to three different services that have that data. I need to tell them which way is the best, or the fastest, or the most accurate, or the most cost-effective. Certainly, cost is a huge concern. If reporters are used to AutoTrack, which is fairly expensive, I have to try to convince them to look at the other services that may not incur a cost per search. That has been really difficult. Reporters want to learn one thing and know that they can always go there. But everything seems to change every six months.

I try to teach reporters to know their sources. If you're searching a newspaper archive, know what years it covers. If you're looking for a story from *The Miami Herald*, or any other Knight Ridder paper, you won't find it on Nexis, unless it's a recent business story that went out over the KRT Business News wire [104]. For other *Herald* stories, you might find abstracts only; you'll have to go to Dialog or NewsLibrary for full-text *Herald* stories. If you want a story from the *Sun-Sentinel* from 1990, you won't find it on Nexis. It will be on Dialog and on the *Sun-Sentinel*'s Web search page [170], which has stories back to 1985, three years before the Dialog archive starts and nine years before the Nexis archive starts. I advise people to look at a source that gives archive dates and coverage, like *Fulltext Sources Online* [230], or the list of newspapers online that I put together two years ago—it needs updating—available on the SLA News Division site [165].

I sometimes find it hard to convince people not to search the Net first when looking for news stories. Dialog and Nexis both claim their database collections are many times bigger than the Internet, and Dow Jones and NewsLibrary also have huge collections of news databases. It's inefficient to spend hours searching for an old news story all over the Net when you can find it quickly and relatively easily in the Web-based search services provided by the traditional online vendors. All these services offer easy date range, story length, and byline searching as well as other specialized features. If you don't have subscription access to news archive databases like Nexis, Dialog, NewsLibrary, or Dow Jones Interactive [48], you can sign up for pay-as-you-go searching. Search for the stories you need and pay for only the ones you want. The cost of two to three dollars per story is certainly reasonable when you need the story. Or try Northern Light [140], where you can retrieve stories from many newspapers and magazines for as little as a dollar per story.

If you must search individual news archives, particularly for papers that don't have archives on one of the commercial services, check that list of online news archives at the SLA News Division site before you start. The list includes coverage dates when available. There may be archives that have not yet been added to this list, so check the Web page of the paper you're looking for, too.

Let's talk about what you can find on the Net that you couldn't find a few years ago. What Internet resources have impressed you the most?

One thing that still boggles my mind is access to government documents. If we needed the text of a bill or law, we'd have to find someone in the legislature to fax it to us, or wait for the book to come from the state legislature. It would come out six months after the legislative session was over, and it might not contain the text of the bill as it passed. We couldn't easily get access to bills and so on from Congress, since the *Herald* doesn't have the budget for all the primary documents that a larger paper can subscribe to. Now, if somebody needs the text of a bill or of a Supreme Court decision, or a primary government document, it's on the Net, and it takes just a few seconds to access.

Do you have any tips for accessing government information on the Web? In the past, there have been so many places to go. Do you rely heavily on bookmarks?

I keep bookmark files on our intranet. On the government page, you can click on "laws" or on "bills" and it will show you the best places to go. I try to list alternatives, but I highlight the ones that I think are the best places to start. Search engines often find what you need, but I still think that you need a catalog to tell you where to go for information. That's part of my job, to create that catalog of resources on the Internet that I know my reporters are going to need. Things keep changing and I try to keep on top of the changes.

Rather than trying to search for things, I try to think about which agency is going to deal with a particular topic and go to that agency's Web page and start looking there. The general search engines are not the answer for government documents. If you don't know what agency to start with, there are some good government-only search engines, such as GovSearch [82] from Northern Light, Uncle Sam from Google [81], and FedWorld [65], that can find things more quickly than using a general search engine.

When you do use a general search engine, what techniques work best for you?

I have better luck with Web-based searches when I start out with the broadest possible search. If I'm searching for a news story in the Web version of Nexis, Dialog or Dow Jones, I do a simple word, phrase, or AND/OR search. If it's a large topic, I limit to the Major Story category, which searches headline and/or lead paragraph. If I get too many hits, I go back and add additional terms, story length qualifiers, and so on.

The same is true in Web search engines. I love AltaVista [7] and know it can do very specialized searches, but in most cases I just put in a few words. If my search contains a phrase, I put it in quotes. Often, I find that the search engines' relevancy ranking quickly finds what I'm looking for; there's no need for complex searches. Searches that are too specific can eliminate citations you want. But evaluating the results requires a bit of intuition, sometimes, to recognize which ones might have the information you want. That comes with practice; if it's not clear, it may be time to try refining the search.

Do you use metasearch engines?

I use metasearch engines mostly for the more obscure searches, such as the name of a person who doesn't happen to be famous, or for information that I think might be buried down within Web pages. When I need to use metasearch engines, I try at least three. In many cases, I get very different results from different engines. I use metasearch engines like MetaCrawler [120], MetaFind [121], and Mamma [115]. Of course, all the search engines keep changing; there's always something new that seems to work better for a while than everything else. Everyone loves Google right now, and I have to admit that sometimes it does get me just exactly what I want.

My current favorite search to test a new search engine is "florida electric chair." When I needed to find out some obscure facts about the chair, most search engines found only news stories. Very few sites have any information about the chair itself. The best info I found came from just one or two search engines, out of the many I tried—and not from metasearches.

If it's a fairly straightforward search and I think there's going to be one Web page that will answer the question, I might just go to AltaVista or HotBot [86] or Lycos [113]. Sometimes I prefer to try the individual search engines separately, even if I have to try two or three of them. It depends on what I'm searching for. I just have this gut feeling about which is going to work.

Isn't that where your bookmarks and intranet guides come into play, so that people don't mush around and waste time searching?

Exactly. I feel strongly that the first thing to do is to find the best directory on a topic. There's always somebody who is an expert, who knows exactly where all the good stuff is. And they've compiled it in a data directory. Go to FindLaw [67], or something similar, if you're looking for legal information. Go to one of the medical directories, like Achoo! [5]. It's sort of like a Yahoo! [206] for health information. There are many new health portals now, but Achoo!'s been around for a long time, and I've gotten used to using it. It's the same with other topics. I've tried to find the *best* directories on many different subjects and list them on the intranet.

How do you deal with the authority and data integrity of materials found on the Internet? How do you teach your reporters to evaluate sources and sites?

I really haven't found that to be a problem. I think reporters are even more skeptical about Web sites than I am. I always hear them saying, "You can't trust this" and "You can't trust that," and "How do you know it's any good?" Obviously, they do a lot of browsing and they like to fool around with strange Web sites. But when they're working, they understand which sources are authoritative or official and which are not.

Our problem is not so much with the Web as with public records. Public records may not be clear on people's identities. There may be two people with the same name, or a similar name, or they may look like they're related but perhaps they're not. We sometimes find records that indicate that two or three other people have used the same social security number. Reporters tend to think there is some kind of conspiracy when, really, it's a clerk entering data and making a mistake, like transposing numbers or something.

We have a lot more difficulty resolving public records questions. A lot of them include dates of birth and social security numbers. But many don't—corporate records, real estate records—they just have a name. So, when there are several people with the same name, there's no way to know for sure if it's the right person. You have to match addresses or do whatever you can. It's like doing a Web search on a name and coming up with several hits: How do you know which records match until you know more about the person?

Have you ever contacted people at a Web site to verify data or to ask questions?

Our reporters do that often. One of the important things I teach them is how to find out who owns a Web site, and who the name is registered to. I'll often check the domain name registration to determine ownership. I go to the bottom of a Web page to look for contact information. If it's a company name that I don't recognize, I might then look for incorporation records to get more information. Many times I'm trying to answer a question from a reporter who wants to get in touch with a company, and it's so annoying to find a Web page with no address or phone number information anywhere.

Do you or the reporters use electronic mailing lists and discussion groups?

Many of us subscribe to NICAR-L [218], the computer-assisted reporting list, and maybe the IRE list [216]. Of course I use the NewsLib list [222] for news researchers and librarians. I teach reporters how to use Deja.com [42] to search for discussion group messages. Most of them don't want to subscribe and read all the messages every day, but they may want to know what somebody's saying today about a story they're working on. If a particular story is going on, say a plane crash, people might want to see what's being said on the aviation lists. I expect that several reporters who cover specific beats, like health or aviation, subscribe to lists on those topics. We often monitor the Cuba newsgroups. After a shooting of a repo man here, the reporter monitored a newsgroup devoted to repossession agents and got some gossipy tips about another agent who might have been involved.

Have you found Deja.com to be a useful resource?

We have used it many times just to see what's being said in certain groups. It was really useful in the story about the TWA Flight 800 crash. Two weeks after the crash, a story was getting out on talk radio, saying that *The Miami Herald* had reported that two Arkansas state troopers were on the plane on their way to being interviewed by *Paris Match*. Somebody called up *The Miami Herald* and asked if the story was true. And we said, "What? What story?"

I'd heard a rumor that the story was on the Net, so I searched Deja.com and found the original message, which had been copied and passed along in several newsgroups. Once I had the original email message, I traced the address through other messages the person had sent, and eventually found a Web page on which he was listed. We discovered that he was a guy who worked on a military base in north Florida, who had lived in Miami once. I sent him email and got a long message back, and several more messages after that, and a reporter called and talked to him. He wouldn't admit sending the original message, but said he believed that whoever did was just "trolling for idiots" to see who would bite. It turned into a front page story, on which I got a byline, explaining how careful you have to be about believing information you find on the Net. I also sent a message to several of the newsgroups explaining that the story wasn't true. It was on its way to becoming another urban legend.

Do you subscribe to any email news alert services?

I subscribe to some "what's new on the Internet" lists but not to any other kind of news alerts. For reporters, I highly recommend services like 1stHeadlines [3] and Yahoo! News Page [209], which go into comprehensive coverage whenever there's a breaking story. They link to the current news and sometimes to relevant Web pages. When there's a breaking story, I try immediately to link to something like that. If it's something where we need to go into great detail, I'll start compiling my own list of links and give that to reporters. Some reporters use Nexis' personal news alert service, which finds new stories on particular topics. That only works for reporters who have a specific beat or are working on a long-term project on a particular topic.

Our reporters and editors are still on our SII editing system software [254], which has continuous feeds from all newswires. They're all used to getting the news off this old computer system, and they're comfortable with that. They're not yet dependent on the Web for breaking news.

How do you personally stay updated on what you have to know?

I check all the "what's new" sites on the Internet constantly. Several places provide compilations of news sites. I go through those at least weekly—things like The Scout Report [220] and the New this Week lists at the Librarian's Index to the Internet [109] site, put together by Carole Leita at the UC Berkeley Library. I check all the lists linked from that site's Keeping up with New Internet Resources list [108]. I check Yahoo!'s What's New [210] daily. I also check Gary Price's Direct Search lists [76] and several others. I get email newsletters from Lexis and Dialog, so I find out about new sources there.

I used to subscribe to journals like *Information Today* [233], *Online* [235], and *EContent* [227], but we've cut paper subscriptions. So, I check their Web sites for new articles. I try to make a point of getting to the Information Today site and other library sites for news. I have a whole page on the intranet just for the information center, and one section contains all the links for library news, including the Information Today link [93], and a link to the News Division of the Special Libraries Association [165].

How do you handle the changing nature of the Internet, the problems of currency and permanence? Is it a problem for you that one day something is there and the next day it might not be?

That's a problem, especially when you're maintaining an intranet with a lot of links on it, which I do. There are different philosophies about intranet links collections. Some believe you should keep the list short. But I think that, if you find something really specific that nobody will need for another six months, you still have to make a link to it, because you're going to waste an awful lot of time trying to find it again. So, I have lots of links on my intranet, and I check them often. I'm always checking the Florida State government pages just to see if there's anything new.

Sometimes, I don't know that things have changed until I try to get to them. But if you know how to trace old links back up to the main page, or to search for a new link, you can usually find it. I've only encountered a couple of sites that have totally disappeared.

We also use software that automates link checking. I use HomeSite from Allaire [249]. It takes a long time to verify all the links on a page. I finish editing a page, turn on that program, and walk away for an hour. But it's worth it, because it really does check all the links and give me a list of bad ones to fix.

What do you find most frustrating about the Internet?

There's always the day that it goes down just as you're really involved in a big story and need something desperately—and a crucial Web page isn't working, or the whole Web is unresponsive and slow. We're using the Web as our primary source. A lot of the big services that we've been using, like Lexis and Dialog and the others, are now on the Web. Sometimes, the complicated structure of those Web sites just doesn't work on some of our PCs; we've got people using PCs that may not be quite powerful enough, or they have older browsers. A lot of great resources on the Internet are evolving and using new technology. It's hard to keep up with that technology when you've got a large company with a lot of computers that need to be upgraded. The more complicated a Web page gets, the greater the chance that it's not going to work for somebody. We can access most of the online services by modem in an emergency, but that doesn't help the reporters who are used to getting the information at their desks.

Given the changes the Web has already wrought—in supporting news organizations as well as becoming a news delivery mechanism—where do you see research

and reporting methods moving over the next few years?

It's hard to say. But one thing I'm seeing that fascinates me is the fact that a lot of reporters and editors are leaving traditional newspapers and news organizations and going to strictly Web sites, like TheStreet.com [173] or APBnews.com [14]. Certainly, I believe that people are always going to want to have a newspaper in their hands. Although I love reading my newspaper at home in the morning, I find myself getting a lot of news off the Web these days. I'll go to *The New York Times*' Web site [133] rather than look for the paper in the newsroom. I have very little interest in television news anymore, unless it's something local, or breaking news that hasn't hit the Web sites yet.

Does your dislike of television relate to the fact that it's not interactive—you don't have control—whereas with a newspaper in hand, with a Web site and browser, with all the other news that you get online, you're in control?

Exactly. When I watch TV now, particularly something like news or sports, I think, "If only I could have a little Web page about this in the corner of the screen, so I could look up those stats or whatever." What's wonderful about the news on the Web is that you can make all those links.

I think the news sites that offer depth are the ones that are going to succeed. I certainly see research as being a big part of that, but so far I don't see researchers involved in the online newspaper products. There may be cases where they've left the newsroom and gone to work for an online venture, but usually not in a research capacity. I think that's going to have to evolve.

Has *The Miami Herald* embraced this transformation to an interactive medium?

We're part of Knight Ridder, and Knight Ridder has a very strong commitment to interactivity. It was one of the first companies to offer newspaper Web pages, and almost all Knight Ridder papers now have Web sites through the Real Cities network [154]. The sites are not just the online edition of the newspaper; they include community directories, entertainment guides, and that sort of thing. We've gotten pretty good at the *Herald* at making all our stories interactive. Now, whenever there's a project or a big story, everybody knows that they've got to contribute to the Web product as well, by putting primary sources online or adding value somehow.

One of the things that almost all newspaper Web pages lack, in my opinion, is the graphic component. Thirty or forty stories in the newspaper on any given day might include photographs, but the Web versions of the stories don't have the photographs. News libraries are developing photo archives but, except in a rare case or two, those archives aren't available on the Web. They haven't developed in many cases into an integrated database of text and photos, but are separate archives that have to be searched separately. And they are only available to newsrooms, not to online customers.

In our newspaper, the online department seems very separate from the newsroom. But there is some synergy, like a calendar listings desk, which is based in our library but enters community calendar information that appears in the newspapers and is also searchable in a database on our Web site. Of course, our text archive is an important component of our Web page, too.

What do you like best about what you do?

I just love the news, and I love being in the middle of a breaking story. A reporter may be calling me from the road asking for a phone number or a quick piece of information. Several other reporters may be working on the same story and need me to identify the information they need as I am gathering it for others. An editor may ask me to collect all the background on a person or topic and maybe put together a chronology. I will try to find all the best Web sites on the topic and throw them onto the intranet so that people have links to follow. It's exciting to be that involved in the news as it's happening.

I feel like a teacher in a lot of ways, because I'm showing people where to go to get information. I like being involved with readers. I really like when I get to write things, like chronologies or explanatory boxes, that get in the paper, where I'm actually speaking to the readers. I wish I could do it more often. But I'm also very happy just helping reporters. It's important to me to help them to do the best job they can, because I admire what they do.

Super Searcher Power Tips

➤ In matching the voter list to the social security death filings, we discovered lots of supposedly dead people who had voted. Many of them proved to be alive, though; it turned out only one "voter" was truly dead. This led us to realize that social security death filing data are not accurate at all.

➤ Computer-assisted reporting can really contribute to a project. With the databases loaded locally, I can pull out large groups of records that match certain criteria. I can't do that with the online databases.

➤ One of my most important research tips is to know your sources. Check out *Fulltext Sources Online* for listings of archive dates and coverage, or the list of newspapers online that I put together on the SLA News Division site.

➤ If you don't have subscription access to news archive databases like Nexis, Dialog, NewsLibrary, or Dow Jones Interactive, you can sign up for pay-as-you go searching. The cost of two to three dollars per story is certainly reasonable when you need the story.

➤ The first thing to do is to find the best directory on a topic. Go to FindLaw, or something similar, if you're looking for legal information. Go to one of the medical directories, like Achoo!.

➤ I highly recommend services like 1stHeadlines and Yahoo! News Page, which go into comprehensive coverage whenever there's a breaking story. They immediately link not only to all the news, but to all the good Web pages.

Michael Wendland

"PC Mike," the High Tech News Hound

Mike Wendland is an award-winning journalist and investigative reporter who has worked in newspapers, TV, radio, and Webcasting. He holds Internet training sessions around the U.S. and is a Fellow of the Poynter Institute for Media Studies. He has authored several books about the Internet.

mike@pcmike.com
www.pcmike.com

You seem to be a ubiquitous journalist. You're in TV, radio, on the Web, in newspapers; you do a column—you're all over the place. Tell me how this happened.

I've been a journalist since I was a kid of twelve and published a hand-stenciled sheet called "Neighborhood News" for my neighbors. I worked my way through college doing news for a little radio station in my hometown. But most of my background is in print journalism. I spent about thirteen years at newspapers, including ten at *The Detroit News*, which at that time was the largest evening newspaper in the country.

In 1980, I went to work for Washington Post-Newsweek Television. I started the first "I" or investigative team at WDIV-TV, the NBC affiliate in Detroit. I headed that up until mid-1998 when I quit to devote all my time to teaching, reporting, and writing about the Internet.

Along the way, in the late '80s and early '90s, I picked up a lot of skills in using computers to do reporting. That expertise turned into a syndicated TV piece called "High Tech Talk," which I've been doing since '94 for all 250 NBC television affiliates. And that led to a series of six books about the Internet, and in '94, it hooked me up with the Poynter Institute [146, see Appendix] and RTNDA [153]—the Radio/TV News Directors Association—and here I am!

I think the neatest thing about being a journalist is that you get paid for satisfying your curiosity. And I'm pretty curious. Another good thing about journalism is that it takes so many different forms. I get really excited learning new things all the time. I've been able to do my work in just about every type of medium there is, including live Webcasts—regular TV shows broadcast live on the Internet.

How did you learn online researching? Did you go to training sessions? Have you worked closely with news librarians?

Learning came out of necessity. No one was an expert when I started. I began with the old Delphi system, which was a text-based online service, and then CompuServe [35] got pretty good. For a while, that was the big rage. I started using it immediately, as newspapers and magazines went online, and as a means of communication with other people who were doing stuff out in the field. Then the Internet and the Web developed, and I was right there in the midst of it all.

My involvement with librarians really came through Nora Paul and the Poynter Institute. I developed a deep respect for what they do. My previous experience with librarians had been that they were basically clip jockeys—at *The Detroit News*, they'd just bring you a clip file. That was about it. When I was with Washington Post-Newsweek Television, there was nobody at the local television station who served as a librarian or archivist. So, I jumped into online research pretty much on my own, and I've used it ever since.

Does someone assist you with research for your books and other writing?

I did a book called *The Wired Journalist* [241] about online research and reporting. After I compiled my list of bookmarks, I hired somebody to go through and check them because, as you know, they go out of date very quickly. But when I'm dealing with online research I need to know it myself. I need to visit Web sites myself.

What tips do you have for handling your bookmarks?

It's very simple. I always travel with my bookmarks. I use them extensively. I organize them using Internet Explorer. I organize everything in files and even subfiles, and I keep them on a floppy disk. I use a computer at Poynter, I have my laptop with me on the road, I have three computers in my home office, and I use a Palm VII for wireless connecting. With the exception of the Palm VII, I have the same bookmarks on every machine. So I keep them on a floppy. The master is on my main computer at home, and every week I save to the floppy and I carry that around. I've used the same system now for four or five years and it's pretty good. The only thing I change, depending on which project I'm working on, is to add some sites to the Links bar at the top of my browser window, so they're easier to get to.

Let's talk about some of your research techniques. When you have an information trail that you want to follow or an article that you want to develop, do you have a method? Where do you begin?

Here's where the librarians don't like me. Nora has a fit every time, but I love to do this at the end of a training session. One of the reasons I like Internet Explorer is that it's so darn convenient. It has a simple feature that allows you to just go to the URL address bar and type in the word "find" followed by however you want to phrase your search. Probably eighty-five percent of the time, that gets me enough to get focused on a search. From there, I'll develop it. I'll use Google [80], which everybody else has fallen in love with lately. There's a product called Copernic [247], which I like because it searches a lot of different online sites and newsgroups at the same time. I also recently started using FAST [63], one of the newer search engines.

Which electronic mailing lists do you find most useful?

The best one all around for me, and it has been for several years now, is CARR-L [212], Elliot Parker's list for Computer Assisted Research and Reporting. Year in and year out, it's been the most responsible and helpful for basic quick journalism research. I could not imagine being without that list.

Because of the nature of what I specialized in—organized crime and corruption and investigations—I've used the NICAR (National Institute of Computer-Assisted Reporting) list [218] and the IRE (Investigative Reporters and Editors) list [216]. I'm currently doing a book on an investment organization, so I subscribe to that organization's mailing list. That generates, in digest form, probably 100 messages a day. But that's temporary; it's just for this book project.

I also get a couple of technology alerts. Wired [225] does a pretty good review. IDG [214] has a good one. I go on and off those lists fairly frequently, when I get tired of seeing the same messages. NewsHub [136] updates and posts technology news every fifteen minutes. That's pretty fresh, and hard to beat.

Have you found the lists useful for people contacts or leads?

Yes, the CARR-L list has helped me develop a pretty good group of friends out there. It's a great way to network and get story ideas, as journalists share their successes and struggles and try to help each other out. I find a lot of story ideas in news-groups, too. I think newsgroups are the equivalent of the person on the street interviews that we do as journalists. It's the person in cyberspace.

That leads me to the notion of the integrity and the authority of the material you're finding. How do you evaluate sources and sites? Do you find this to be a problem?

Yes, I sure do. A good journalist is skeptical by nature, so you don't necessarily believe everything you read. The second thing you learn is that everybody's got an agenda, and that includes the big, supposedly legitimate, portal sites like MSNBC [125] and CNN.com [34], as well as the NRA Web site [141], or any of the others. Everybody's got an agenda.

I tend to ask, first, do I know who these people are? Can I pick up the phone and get ahold of somebody? Or can I get in a car and drive to an address? Is it a post office box? Can I contact them through the site?

A couple of times a week, I do a Whois [203] search to see who owns a domain name. It never ceases to amaze me how some big sites just assume that people know who they are. It makes it very difficult to reach them. If they make it difficult to pick up the phone and reach them, it tells me that there's a problem there, some way or another. There's a reason they don't want people to find them.

Then the next question is, how current is the information? Is the site updated regularly? When I look at a Web site, I usually just take down whatever information I see, and then I try to call somebody and ask them to amplify on whatever point it is I'm looking at. I look at the Web as a real interesting efficiency improver, I guess. You still have to go out and knock on a door or pick up a phone and talk to somebody most of the time.

I understand that you've won some Emmys over the years, and probably some other writing

awards. Do you have a favorite example of a project that involved in-depth research?

Yes, I've got an easy one and a hard one. Just to show you what a difference the Internet has made, about four or five years ago I did a terrific story about the theft of dogs. It was a great story, because it's apparent that there are dog-stealing rings that roam all over the country and sometimes literally steal dogs right from their leashes in their back yards. They move around a region of the country and invariably end up at these so-called dog auctions that are held in a number of southern states. Dogs are put in cages and these bunchers, as they're called, bring the dogs that they've stolen, or sometimes bought from animal pounds, to these dog auctions. Then animal dealers, who are licensed by the U.S. Department of Agriculture, come in and buy these dogs from the bunchers and sell them to universities and hospitals and very prestigious organizations for medical research. We went under cover all over the country, and cracked this so-called "dog mafia."

I had a lot of difficulty getting the documents that traced which research sites and universities were buying dogs for research, and the government paperwork that would show who sold them the animals. The records were there, but only in hardcopy paper form. Then I researched what kinds of complaints were on file about these animal dealers. It took three or four months to do the story, and then about two months just to gather the paperwork. It was all handwritten paper copies from the USDA. You go through and enter the data by hand. This was in '95 or '96.

In '98, I looked into the story again, but by this time, all those files, all those forms were online at the USDA [185]. So, I just logged on and downloaded them, did my sorts, and identified which animal dealers had the most complaints, what the complaint status was, where they were selling their animals, where they were getting them from. It was all there. In two hours, literally, I had completed the work that had taken me at least two months to do before. That's one of my best examples of what a difference the Internet makes.

Now I'll mention an example at a simpler level. This doesn't have anything to do with online research *per se*; it's more about the technology. I was covering a Mafia trial. In court, they announced that a hit man was going to come and testify in Detroit. I was right in the courtroom and the only reporter there at that time, so it was a great scoop for me. This guy was a notorious hit man, and had confessed to I think dozens of murders on the East Coast, and had a pretty extensive record. The only problem was that I was in television, and I needed a picture of this guy, but I didn't have any way to get one. So, I called a friend who worked for the *Village Voice*. He had a picture of this guy on file, because they'd done a story on him when he testified there. He just scanned the picture in and emailed it to me. I was able to videotape it right off the TV screen, and then edit the guy's picture in my reporting package. These things are so simple to do, but very few people do them. They will wait for somebody to mail those pictures, or FedEx them. The Internet makes it so convenient.

You mentioned the USDA. We seem to have a lot more access to government information than ever before.

Finally, yes. The government agencies were very reluctant to accept the Internet, and only came to it kicking and screaming, until about two years ago. But now, they're really embracing it. They would rather release stuff on the Internet. It saves a lot in printing costs. It saves time for people who don't have to go look up hard copies anymore. Almost every agency is rushing to put their stuff into electronic archives. For researchers, that's great.

It has been tough to navigate around on the government sites. Have you looked at GovSearch [82] from Northern Light?

Yes, I think that is really so exciting. It's going to be one of the high destination sites. Another great site is Deja.com [42], which lets you search all the different newsgroups. It's one of the best-kept secrets on the Internet; it's terrific for quickly background-ing people. I did stories on the Heaven's Gate cult where I was able to trace the proselytization that these cultists were doing all around the country. I could do a wildcard author search. If some-one has ever posted a message in an Internet newsgroup, you can find it here. Deja.com lets you retrieve newsgroup posts by typing in the name of a person or their email address. Embarrassing personal details and angry tirades written long ago—back to the mid-'90s—can come back to haunt somebody.

Besides increased access to government information, what can you find on the Net that you couldn't just a few years ago?

The people finder sites, such as Switchboard [171], are a good example. Mapping software, such as MapQuest [117]. Reverse telephone look-ups, like that available from AnyWho [13]. Movie schedules. Streaming video news, such as Fox News [70] or Bloomberg Business Video [26]. The list keeps growing. The Internet makes getting information so much more efficient.

Do you use any of the specialized news search engines?

I do a site about high-tech and computer news for consumers, called PCMike.com [142]; it's updated about three or four times a day. I've used a service called NewsHub [136], which is a news spider that you can stick on your own Web site if you work out a deal with them. At the Poynter site, Poynter.org, we use Autonomy [245] software to help journalists monitor their beats and stay informed.

One of my favorite examples, and one of my favorite sites in the whole Internet, is a site called Cyber Paperboy [38]. It's a mass of links to breaking news and entertainment stories, and it's always updated. But what is really cool about this site, I think, is who does it. This is *not* a journalist. This is not a guy who has a background in research. This is an auto mechanic who is the owner of DJ's Strut

& Brake Shop in Clawson, Michigan! He just loves the Internet. I did a story on him for NBC. In the middle of his brake jobs, he'll stop, go wash the grease off his hands, and jump on the Web to update the links to news stories all over the country.

The thing that's amazing is that this guy often scoops MSNBC or CNN. He's competing with the big guys. It's a fascinating site. I love to use it as an example when I talk with journalists. I tell them that, unless you are really comfortable in this medium, you are obsolete, because DJ's Strut & Brake Shop can do just as good a job as you can at finding this stuff. You have to give the news that much more depth and perspective to make it worthwhile, because this guy is beating you.

What advice do you give journalists for staying on top of things?

I've been training journalists for five years now. I do training at Poynter and I do it as a consultant around the country. I do research workshops on how to use the Internet. I think that journalists, and broadcast journalists in particular, are behind the rest of the public in mastering searching techniques on the Internet. Now, I'm not talking about all of them. Obviously some journalists are very good at research. But, so many of them are reluctant to learn something new, and they look at this as, "Yeah, that's nice, but I don't have the time to learn it."

But five U.S. cities now have more than fifty percent Internet penetration in terms of Net access at home. Broadband will change everything. The Internet is truly the most significant communication medium that we have ever developed. If journalists are not masters of this incredibly powerful tool, they're going to give it up to people like the Cyber Paperboy.

In an age when anyone can be a publisher, anyone can be a researcher, and anyone can be a journalist, the real trick to set yourself

apart as a journalist must be your credibility— and what else?

Your credibility *and* your ability to sift through and go deeper. What we bring to it is our judgment as a news professional. That can never be lost. But we have to operate on Internet speed now, rather than newspaper speed. When I first started in newspapers, we had six editions a day. That went down to four, and then three, and then, I'd say for most papers, two. How could you compete with TV and radio? We now have Internet speed, which is updated minute by minute. And we have to think in those terms.

But does that impact the time and care that people take to verify and make sure of the accuracy of their sources?

I don't think the public knows, or has the ability to discern, what is a reliable source and what is not a reliable source. On the Internet, anybody can look pretty reliable. The danger I see is that, in this age of information on demand, without some professional standards out there to take the lead and direct this technology and move it forward, we're going to lose our edge to those who are just technology people—those who know how to use and leverage technology. As journalists, we're not as deeply involved as we need to be in the medium itself. The Internet is not just a supplement to our newspaper or our television station, it is indeed a medium all by itself. In the near future—five years—it will be more powerful, more influential, and more dominant than radio, or TV, or print. That's my prediction.

You talk about being able to find most of what you want on the Net, but what about the so-called "invisible Web"—the sites that are password-protected or fee-based, with hidden databases that the regular search engines don't

touch? Do you feel that you're missing chunks of information?

No, I don't. For what I have needed, I can't think of anything that I have not been able to find. I have done a little bit with Lexis-Nexis [106] in the past, but I don't subscribe to any paid services on my own. I'm sure there's other stuff out there, but I just don't have time to look for it all. To me, it's a matter of being efficient and getting information as quickly as I can.

I start with a pretty broad search of the Web and then quickly narrow it down as I see how that broad one comes back. More often than not, the Internet Explorer "Find" or the Google "Search" gives me what I'm looking for in the first five or ten hits, or it leads me to it. Once you get to a fairly good site, look at the links that it lists. Often, I'll find really great obscure stuff that none of the search engines pick up, by going to a site and looking at what it links to.

But I usually search in broad sweeps for story background rather than for individual specific facts. I seldom need to know how many people live in Afghanistan. I would be more interested in the use of boy soldiers in Afghanistan. I can pretty much find that in just a couple of minutes. A librarian or researcher may need to do more precise fact searching than the broad kind of stuff I do. That's why I don't need to use those resources as deeply. Knowing they're there is great, and I'm sure the time will come when I do need them. At this point, it's not that hard to find information anymore.

What do you think about news organizations that encourage interactions between their reporters and readers through the Web? Will that have a positive or a negative impact on the work that goes into reporting?

If you are talking about listing a reporter's email address, I think that's a pretty good tool. I know of a reporter in Minnesota who broke a big story only because he had an email address. He started getting anonymous email tips that led to a murder confession in a very sensational case. After the story broke, he asked the person, "Why did you contact me?" And the guy said, "Because you had an email address."

We do need to talk to people who read and see our stories. There are journalists who don't like it when the paper runs their phone number or their email address. In fact, they invariably will get calls from people with agendas. But that's what we're supposed to do. If you're offended by getting all these calls for your stories, then get out of the business. People should have the right to reach you. I like that. I think it involves you in the story. It always leads to better relations with the people who consume our news products. And it leads to follow-up stories.

Other than wishing for unlimited bandwidth for all of us, what one wonderful improvement in searching would you like to see?

The first thing I want is "instant on." I'm so sick of computers that take two to three minutes to boot up. If we had computers that were instantly on and instantly connected, that would help a lot.

I'd like something a little better than Alexa [6] to get a profile of a Web site. I would love a little box to come up that says this site is owned by so-and-so at this address with this telephone number, and the site has been in existence since this date. I'd like some easy way to identify site ownership.

A lot of people are speculating about the newsroom of the future. What do you see as possible changes in research and reporting methods?

When I talk to reporters, I always start my sessions by asking them, "How many of you have a pager? Put your hand up. Just leave your hand there." And then, "How many of you have a cell phone? Put your hand up. How many of you have a laptop with

America Online or whatever you subscribe to?" And then I ask them, "How many of you had these things five years ago?" And, almost all the hands go down. Just think of where we're going to be in five years. Think what it would be like without pagers and cell phones today.

I carry around with me now the most significant break-through I've seen—the Palm VII. There's also the Handspring Visor [83], which has the power that a mainframe computer had ten years ago. I can access my email walking down the street. I'm driving in a car and I can get on MapQuest and get directions to wherever I'm going.

I also get newsfeeds on my Palm VII. I've got ABC News [4], I've got *The Wall Street Journal* [197], I've got Wired News. All these things are right up-to-date. I can do a people search through a little Yahoo! [206] function, get phone numbers of neighbors of the news scene I'm going to. If traffic's bad, I can punch on this thing while I'm driving down the road, and it will give me up-to-date traffic reports. It's amazing. It's still a little too costly for most of us. But I think we will see much more power-ful compact devices that we will all carry in our purse or shirt pocket or wherever, that will hook up with our office computers. It will be a pager, a cell phone, and more. Nokia is coming out with a Palm Pilot in a Nokia telephone. Incredible. I couldn't get along without my Palm Pilot now.

I'll play devil's advocate and ask, "Doesn't something like that reduce news to simply headlines?"

Well, that's really what news is, just the headlines right now. That's the way we're all doing it—television, radio, newspapers. What this device does is make my life a whole lot more efficient. I can punch it up and find out the latest development on what-ever story I'm working on. I can get directions to the location that I'm going to. I can send an email or transmit a photo back to the office. I can take a personal computer and actually do a live update from the scene. That's what I'm talking about. It keeps me informed. It points me in the right direction to go out and dig for the more substantive things that make for good journalism.

I've done work recently where I go out with a digital camera, a video camera, a laptop, and a cell phone. I don't need a microwave truck anymore. I don't need a satellite truck. I can hook up anywhere in the world and send pictures and audio back to be put on the air. That is what the future holds. These devices will just get smaller and smaller and more all-purpose. We'll always be publishing. And we'll always be reporting.

The news of the future is going to be on a little screen that we'll carry around with us in our pocket or have hanging overhead at our desk. Maybe when we get home at the end of the day, we punch a button and out prints a newspaper, if we want, so we can take some paper with us to the chair. Or, maybe we just watch it on a screen. But that's the way it's going to be. And it's going to be updated constantly. Hourly. Moment by moment. I think it's a pretty exciting time to be a journalist. It really is.

Especially one who covers these kinds of high-tech developments, right?

I think so. I'm having a ball. Most of my friends have quit the business or are burned out, but I just get more and more excited about it every day.

Super Searcher Power Tips

➤ I always travel with my bookmarks. I organize them using Internet Explorer. I organize everything in files and even subfiles, and I keep them on a floppy disk.

➤ Internet Explorer has a simple feature that allows you to just go to the URL address bar and type in the word "find" followed by however you want to phrase your search. Probably eighty-five percent of the time, that gets me enough to get focused on a search. From there, I'll develop it.

➤ The best list for me is CARR-L, Elliot Parker's list for Computer Assisted Research and Reporting. It has been the most responsible and helpful for doing basic quick journalism research. I could not imagine being without it.

➤ A good journalist is skeptical by nature, so you don't necessarily believe anything you read. Everybody's got an agenda, and that includes the big, supposedly legitimate, portal sites.

➤ Unless you are really comfortable on the Internet, you are obsolete, because DJ's Strut & Brake Shop can do just as good a job as you can at finding this stuff. You have to give the news that much more depth and perspective to make it worthwhile.

➤ Once you get to a fairly good site, look at the sites that it links to. Often, I'll find really great obscure stuff that none of the search engines pick up by going to a site and looking at what it links to.

Kee Malesky

National Public Radio's Voice of Research Expertise

Kee Malesky is Reference Librarian at National Public Radio. She received an MSLS from Catholic University of America in 1986. She is active in the Special Libraries Association News Division and D.C. Chapter, and in Beta Phi Mu, the honor society for library science. She teaches Humanities Reference at CUA's School of Library and Information Science.

kmalesky@npr.org
www.npr.org

Tell me a little about your background.

I worked as an administrator for NPR before I ever thought of getting my library degree. I then had two different library jobs with NPR, during and after graduate school, including cataloging tapes of radio programs, and finally moved into a position in the News reference library in March 1990.

How did you get into doing Internet research?

We've always used the traditional commercial online services. We began to use the Internet in the pre-Web, pre-graphics days, though we did not have access to very many resources. But in the last five years, there's been a rapid change in the way the whole organization uses technology and therefore in the kind of information the Library is able to supply.

The Internet became an essential element in providing good information support for the News division. We're responsible not just to News, but to the entire company. Therefore, the type of information we search for covers questions from the corporate division, from the Distribution folks who run the satellite system, and from the HR department that researches benefits coverage. We have to serve a large number of people, and still with rather limited resources compared to what you'll find in other news organizations.

What is the relationship of the library with the news department and the reporters? Do you have a team approach?

We are part of the News & Information department and report to that vice president. Our relationship with reporters, editors, producers, and editorial assistants is very, very close. I think in some ways that's because we have a small staff compared to many news organizations. There are really just two and a half people to staff the Reference Library seven days a week, so people come to rely on us at a very personal level. I work alone on Saturdays and Sundays, so you can imagine the kind of day I had, for example, with the EgyptAir plane crash. I got a call at 5:30 in the morning suggesting that I come in early. I spent the whole day answering plane crash questions for reporters, preparing fact sheets, talking to editors and producers about what they would need for the next news cycle. So, yes, it is a real team effort.

If a reporter is working on something in advance, maybe to pitch a series idea, or to investigate an industry, he might start by seeing if we have a clip file, because we still clip the newspapers every day. It's a good place to start to research story ideas. Then we might do a search of commercial databases. If the topic has anything to do with business or industry, we might run a Dow Jones [48, see Appendix] search and see what kind of information comes up.

We're also very much involved in helping reporters identify experts that they can interview. Of course, there are many ways to do that. We might simply find articles in which people are quoted. I would do a full-text search in a news database using terms like "university" or "professor;" that way I'm likely to find people being quoted on one or another side of an issue. Beyond that, we use directories of universities and think tanks, and books such as the *Encyclopedia of Associations* [228] and similar resources that help us identify organizations that represent different points of view. We work directly with the reporter, using print and online resources.

Then there's fact checking, which is sometimes done under pressure of a really tight deadline. Maybe an editor is reading a reporter's script, and the introduction says, "Ninety percent of Americans have spanked their children." He doesn't know that to be a fact, so he'll call the library and ask, "Can we find a poll that says that?" And, maybe we can't, or maybe we find a poll that's so small and local that it isn't appropriate to make such a big deal out of it, so the editor rewrites the sentence. We do lots of basic fact checking, such as the exact date something happened, so that we don't just say "recently."

Do the reporters or editors do research themselves, and are you training and working with them?

Yes to both. These are interesting questions—how closely do we work together, and how is that changing? The Internet has had a tremendous impact here—in both positive and negative ways. It isn't good for people to think that everything in the world is available free on the Web. I do see people wasting lots of time with poor search strategies, or coming up with things that are not usable because we have no idea what authority is behind them. These kinds of issues concern us.

But the reality is that the lines are blurring between what a reporter does—or the editorial assistants or the other people in the newsroom—versus what the librarians do. Part of that is because librarians now have easier access to more primary material. You don't have to order a report from the Government Printing Office and wait six weeks, which is not realistic for a journalist. Now we might find the report online [191]. Or we can contact experts and reputable organizations directly and gain from differing points of view. The Internet is invaluable for that.

We find that we're putting together better "information packages" in response to the questions that we get. When we only had Nexis [106], we would say, "Okay, we can get you what other journalists have done on this subject." Now, in addition to that, we can get at more primary material. For example, a reporter from the foreign desk is being sent to a country she's not familiar with. I'm going to give her the *CIA World Fact Book* [32] report on that country. I'll check to see whether that government has a Web site with some interesting historical background. Through the State Department [195], I might be able to find some very good material from the U.S. Embassy in that country. That's in addition to going into Dow Jones and pulling some stories about the economic situation in the country, or profiles of major businesses there. I could also go into Nexis and run a search in the travel sections of newspapers and pull out some interesting feature ideas. I might find some analytical articles in academic journals from EBSCO*host* [51].

Some of these searches the reporters can do, and want to do, for themselves. We're now able to provide much broader and much more in-depth information—at least for a small and under-resourced organization like NPR—than we were able to do just five years ago.

How much research are reporters actually doing themselves?

It depends on the individual reporter. Some people don't feel terribly inclined to poke around on the Web and waste time. That's fine. We do lots of training. We started out with a very basic program—teaching people how to use Netscape, how to move around with the browser, what "graphical user interface" means, what the Internet is—and then we let them play around with it on their own. On the NPR intranet, we have some collections of

Web links arranged by subject area. So the science reporters can go and find some things there, the cultural desk can find resources in the arts and humanities, and so on. We are currently training staff to use Lexis-Nexis Universe [107] or Dow Jones Interactive [48].

Of course, my basic concern is this: If it's a full-time job to be a reporter, to keep up with your beat and your assignment, and it's a full-time job for me as a librarian to keep up with the rapid changes in the technological environment, how can any one person do both things? So, I think reporters will continue to rely on librarians. But it is inevitable that they will increasingly use electronic resources. We find ourselves doing more training and more follow-up on that training. I don't want to be reduced to just a trainer, and I don't want to eliminate my job as a librarian. I really don't see that happening, though, certainly not at NPR, because many people feel they don't have the time, the interest, or the skills to do research themselves except on a very limited basis, such as finding a phone number. I think we will continue to be a very important part of the whole editorial process.

But, there are reporters, particularly in the sciences, for example, who are *very* computer savvy. Our technology and computer industry reporters have all kinds of online sources—usually the free sites that you find on the Web—that they use pretty regularly. Some individual reporters and editors subscribe to update services within their areas, or they get on newsgroups that relate to their assignments, or they use other specialized resources, fee-based or not.

Now that most of the commercial databases are moving to browser-based systems, we have been debating—as has the news library world in general—allowing reporters to do that kind of research for themselves. I find even more problems with that. There are differences between search commands and strategy on Nexis, Dow Jones, Dialog [44] and EBSCO, which are the main systems that we rely on. Now that these systems are on the Web, they're being tweaked and reorganized at least occasionally. To keep up with all that and to be a really good searcher is a big task.

It's taken me fifteen years to develop these skills. If I sit down for an hour or two with reporters, it is just not possible for me to tell them everything I know in that time.

Do you set up alerts on any of those commercial services that automatically go to the reporters?

Yes, but we limit the access. Dow Jones Interactive is available basically to the Business Desk and the corporate people in Development and Finance. Because we have a flat-fee subscription to Lexis-Nexis Universe (LNU), we've been offering it to anyone in the News department who wants to learn it. Some of them are very successful. Others sit through the training and at the end say, "Nope, this is not for me, I don't want to do it." And I say, "That's fine. Just call us and we'll figure out how to find what you need." But some News staff do like to use it themselves.

One of the attractive features of LNU is what they call "Personal News." I show staff how to construct a search and then have Personal News alert them to anything new that fits those criteria. It's great if someone has a lead on a story that hasn't been published or aired anywhere yet. Or, as I tell them, "You're going on vacation for a week, or you've been pulled off your main assignment to work on this breaking news. You don't want to miss what's going to come out in the next week or so. So your choice is to read every newspaper in the world every single day, or ask Nexis to do that for you." They love that. I see lots of people using it. We use Personal News ourselves for the same kind of thing. If we know something is likely to be announced in the next few days, we can just ask Lexis-Nexis to alert us when it's published.

Do you participate in any newsgroups or discussion lists?

We don't use chat groups or newsgroups in the Library, but we do use mailing lists. I consider them as important for research as any other electronic resource. For example, we were maybe halfway through the impeachment process early in 1999, and the managing editor wanted to know what was on the front page of newspapers around the U.S. on the last day before Monica Lewinsky hit the headlines. If I had had an unlimited amount of time, I probably could have coaxed front-page stories out of Nexis. But it's not that easy to say, "Show me page one," because different papers number things in different ways, and "page one" is not an easy search term—and it's not usually something you need to do. So, rather than spending time poking around and guessing, I went right to a mailing list. NewsLib [222] has more than 1,200 subscribers, mostly in news libraries, and many of them are members of the SLA News Division [165]. I just put a message out saying that I'd like to see headlines for January 18th, 1998; I don't need the full stories, just headlines. I figured each library would have access to its own computer in a way that would make it very easy to do that. And sure enough, in less than an hour, I had been faxed dozens of pages with the headlines for that date. I brought them to the managing editor, who was just floored. She thought it was going to take me a few days to put together, and maybe I'd come up with five or six, but I had dozens in less than an hour. Relying on other librarians for that kind of networking and help is so much easier now; you can just send a message to hundreds of people at once, and then sit back and wait for the responses.

I'm also a member of Stumpers-L [224], which is an international mailing list for asking difficult reference questions. The participants are from public libraries, for the most part, but include all kinds of interesting people worldwide. Stumpers is good for the kinds of resources that NPR doesn't have, that I know will likely be in a public library. For example, when I need the lyrics to a song, I'll post a message to Stumpers, and people with good collections of sheet music and lyrics will be able to fax me something in just a few minutes.

So, people are an important component of the whole Internet scene. They remain a very vital source.

Yes! Isn't that nice? The electronic resources make it so much easier to get in touch with people, even with people you don't know. I could have done that Lewinsky project by phone—started with my SLA News Division directory and just called libraries all over the country and asked them to tell me what their headlines were—but that would have taken quite a lot of time. Instead it took two minutes to type up a message, send it out, and just sit back and wait for the answers. It's a wonderful resource. Discussion lists are a very important part of the technological change we're experiencing. Being active on the appropriate lists is an important way to keep up with resources, policies, and issues as well.

When information is available in a number of places—on the commercial online services, or from three or four different Web-based services for free—how do you decide where to get it?

We start with the commercial databases that we subscribe to—Lexis-Nexis, Dow Jones, Dialog, and EBSCO*host*. If I know a particular publication is available in one or more of those systems, the decision may then be based on what kind of search it is. If it's related to business and industry, I will probably go into Dow Jones because I will want *The Wall Street Journal*, which is not in Nexis. I will sometimes use Dow Jones, too, because it is easier to search a group of state newspapers than it is in Lexis-Nexis. If I need a Supreme Court decision, I can use Lexis-Nexis Universe or go to Cornell University's Web page [36].

Wouldn't you go first to a service where you have a flat-fee subscription rather than incurring an additional cost?

Yes, especially if I suspect that I will have to try my search several different ways. When I have no sense of what's out there already, whether anybody has written on the subject, I may have to keep modifying my search—changing the number of synonyms, their proximity, whatever. In a flat-fee database, you don't worry about the clock ticking or costs mounting for every little modification. That's one of the reasons we let the reporters use flat-fee services; if the phone rings in the middle of their search, I don't want them to worry. Go ahead, take your phone call. Your search will still be there when you're done. In the past, our entire explanation of why we didn't let reporters do any database searching was because of the cost involved. The clock was always ticking.

But it's also true that if somebody wants today's *New York Times*, they should know to go to the Web site [133] and just find it there. Maybe a reporter in another country cannot go out and purchase the paper, but needs to see what the *Times* said about what's going on there. I can email from the Web site, or print it out and fax it to her.

Another example: We can now do in Lexis-Nexis Universe many of the same things we can do at the Library of Congress site, Thomas [174], in terms of bill tracking and getting the text of legislation. I tell the reporters to continue using Thomas if they're familiar with it, because it's completely free and the same information is there.

Are you experiencing any management pressure to eliminate some of the fee-based services because they think everything is on the Internet?

No. It's not really a budgetary question for us because there's no real money involved. All of our online searching is what we call a "trade-out." Dialog, EBSCO*host*, Dow Jones, and Lexis-Nexis get on-air funding credits in exchange for giving us a certain amount of access. So, they come up with an amount of service per year that they're willing to let us use. As long as we stay within that limit, it's not a budgetary issue. If those relationships were to expire, I don't know what we would do. We're doing half a million dollars of online searching a year, and I don't see how we could replace that if these relationships suddenly ended. So, it's very important to us to maintain those relationships.

You mentioned some kinds of research that you can do on the Net that you couldn't do before, or couldn't do as easily. What else have you been able to get on the Internet that you couldn't get in the past?

I think it started with phone directories. An especially big challenge for me on the weekends is to find people at home, because they're not in their offices. Having worldwide phone directories has been a life-saver for me. When John Kennedy Jr.'s plane went down, I got a call at home late that Sunday night. The reporter had come up with the name of the man who owned the plane before Kennedy. He wanted to contact him about the maintenance history of the plane. He had the name and he knew he lived somewhere in New Jersey. But directory assistance isn't much help if you don't know the city. The reporter asked me if there was any way we could find him. I said, "Well, if he owns a plane in New Jersey he probably owns a house there, too." So we went into the Public Records Asset Locator section of Lexis-Nexis Universe and searched the man's name in New Jersey. Up came his house; there's his address. So we took the address and went into the reverse search at AnyWho [13], and found his phone number. So, in just five or ten minutes, he had something that, on a Sunday night, would have been impossible to find at all, or would have taken a huge amount of time.

Other kinds of resources we couldn't get before include fast and easy access to government statistics, the text of United Nations resolutions, and academic and research organizations and all the great material they provide. We were sending a new reporter over to Northern Ireland to cover the peace talks there.

I was able to tell her how to find the complete text of the Good Friday Accords at the Web page of the Irish government [100]. She would then know whether provisions were being violated, and whether the position of a particular side was reasonable in terms of the language of the accord, instead of just reading articles that interpreted the agreement.

How do you gather your bookmarks and how do you keep track of them?

I take the advice I read in *Secrets of the Super Net Searchers* [239]: Avoid doing too much blind searching and develop good collections of bookmarks. While researching a query, you often stumble on sites that you know will be useful again. I add bookmarks all the time, then try to go back when it's "quiet" and investigate and evaluate them further. I get a lot of good URLs from people recommending things on mailing lists or in answers to posted questions. Especially with search engines, when people find one they like, they usually like to tell everybody about it. But it's a matter of finding the time to check them out, to read reports on the Web, or in magazines such as *PC World* [236] or *Searcher* [237], that discuss search engines and how well they work.

I organize my bookmark folders by broad subject: U.S. Government, Arts, Language, Sports, etc. I don't bookmark lots of search engines, and I advise people not to try to learn them all. Select a few good ones and learn to use them well. I like AltaVista Advanced [8] because it seems to use the principles of Boolean logic most similarly to the way librarians have always used them. It bothers me to have to learn completely different search concepts for all these search engines. I think it's unfortunate that there's so little standardization and that it doesn't seem that the people designing most of them are talking to librarians for advice.

Do you ever use metasearch engines, or do you tend to go for more specialized sites or search engines for particular types of information?

I don't try very many different search engines, even though I am aware that the overlap among them is not that large. It depends on what kind of results I'm getting, how much depth and breadth the reporter wants, and how much time I have to spend on a particular question.

I do like to have some good metapages. Barbara Gellis Shapiro, who was a news librarian at a paper in Florida, put together a great site for journalists [21]. There are a few others like that. A couple of academics have put together big, no-frills collections of links to all kinds of things. One example is Needle in a CyberStack [132].

Sometimes I use a directory like Yahoo! [206], which I know has lots of information in, say, the arts and humanities, when I might be looking for a dictionary of terminology in the visual arts. One reason to use the Web for a question like that is that you're likely to get nice color pictures to look at as examples. Using an index like Yahoo! and going through its links in the arts will very quickly take you to those kinds of resources. That's helpful with sites that I don't use very often and haven't bookmarked.

I do find that you have to go back to your bookmarks every once in a while and check to see if they're still there and if they've changed in any significant way, so that when you need them on deadline, you're not going to say, "Uh oh, this isn't what it was the last time I used it." That's another part of our responsibility for maintaining current awareness—checking to see if our links are still hot, or if they have moved or disappeared.

That brings up the issue of transitory information on the Internet: Things change, they disappear. You don't know who put them up. How do you deal with data integrity and authority on the Internet? How do you talk to reporters about evaluating sources and sites? What sort of checking do you go through?

I think this may be a little easier for us in the news world than for corporate librarians. We should be able to assume that journalists are careful about these things, that they are not going to take a document with no name on it and assume that the content is valid just because it came from the Internet. But we do give them specific warnings: Just because a page says "updated today" doesn't mean that the particular piece of information you're pulling out of that page is current today. Just because an address has .*edu* in it certainly doesn't mean it has any academic authority behind it, because practically anybody can get a page at a university and do anything they want with it. If you have no idea what this organization is, look for a button that says "who we are" and get some idea of who is behind the site. So, we remind reporters of some of these caveats.

In our training sessions and in meetings I've had with public radio news directors on how they might use the Internet at their local stations, we have recommended tutorials on the Web designed for journalists, such as those at Widener [56] and UCLA [178], that walk them through these kinds of questions and concerns.

Journalists certainly are not immune to being hoaxed, or caught at deadline using something that is not valid or that turns out to be a complete mistake. Remember after the TWA 800 crash, Pierre Salinger said he found a document on the Web that proved the plane had been shot down accidentally by a Navy missile. That was a document that had been floating around absolutely unattributed. I had seen it earlier, so I knew what he was referring to. Of course, an editor came in and said, "I want to find that document." So, I did a search on "TWA" and "missile" and "naval," and up popped maybe five documents. The second one was indeed what Pierre Salinger had been looking at, which most other journalists had said was just a hoax. No one could identify the sender, and it wasn't from any sort of reputable source.

So, the Internet has made things complicated, which I guess happens with most important changes. For the most part, the benefits are overwhelming, but we do have to be cautious.

There's also the complacency of thinking that everything is there and the Web can answer every question. That's certainly not true now, and I don't know if it'll ever be true.

Do you have any favorite search tips that you give your staff?

One of my search tips is to remind News staff that it's often a two- or three- or four-step process to come up with an answer to a question. Sometimes a print source might be the best place to start—for example, when we're trying to track down a person. If they're looking for John Smith in Manhattan, I'm not going to go right to the phone directories. But maybe *Who's Who* [240] will tell me his middle initial or his spouse's name, and maybe the phone is listed under her name. Or I'll check the Yahoo! PeopleFinder, which seems to know everybody who lives in your house. That's how I figured out which Stephen Jay Gould we wanted, of all the Stephen Goulds listed in Massachusetts. *Who's Who* told me his wife's and his son's names, and then Yahoo! PeopleFinder had them listed.

Recently, we were looking for a particular expert on Chechnya who we thought lived in London. I looked in the online London phone book [2] and he didn't seem to be there. I did a byline search to see where he wrote, and I found him at the *Financial Times* and *The Washington Quarterly*. So I called the people here in Washington. They couldn't help me. We had his book on Chechnya, so I looked through the acknowledgments. He mentioned a woman in Washington who had been very generous in sharing her knowledge of Chechnya. I had no idea who this woman was, but she was listed in the phone book in a Washington suburb. So, I called her. She had his home phone number in London and she gave it to me, and we were able to call him. So, I needed human, print, and Internet resources to be able to do that research.

Another tip is to be proactive. You know ahead of time when the Nobel Prizes are going to be awarded, so if you don't already have the Nobel site [139] bookmarked, don't wait until that morning to try to find it. Find it in advance, and let your reporter, your newscaster, whoever, also know about it. For the Tony Awards [176], you could go to the Web page, and as the awards were being announced, a star would appear next to the winner's name.

It takes creative thinking to see how all the research pieces come together.

Oh, I think so. The successful news librarian these days, in addition to being creative, has to be fast. Sometimes it's a matter not just of *where* to find this information, but where to find it really quickly. That's often when I turn to a book. A reporter calls from Capitol Hill and is going on the air in a few minutes to report on the debate about going into Kosovo. He wants to compare that to the vote on the Persian Gulf War. I'm not going to dial into an online source at that point; I'm going to go to *Facts on File* [229] on the shelf. In less than a minute, I was able to give him the vote count and a bit of description of what the debate had been like. There he was on the air five minutes later, saying what I had just told him.

So, reality will always dictate whether you go to print or electronic sources. I certainly could have found that information online in lots of places—including *Facts on File* itself; it's in Lexis-Nexis Universe. But it's still faster, in many circumstances, to go to a book or a magazine or a clip file.

Reporters have always felt time pressure: Get the story out before the newspaper goes to print or the news broadcast is scheduled to air. But the Internet has fostered an increased sense of urgency, with the move to 24/7 and real-time news. Have you felt that pressure as a researcher, and does it influence what you do?

Sometimes it does. We feel pressure to find something as soon as we hear "It's on the Web!" *The Wall Street Journal* [197] broke a story related to the Clinton investigations on its Web page late one Friday, and of course our reporter wanted to see it. She didn't want to go on the air just talking about it based on what we were seeing on the wires; she wanted to read the actual story. At that point, we didn't have access to WSJ.com, which was completely different from Dow Jones Interactive, and we were going crazy trying to get access to the site at that moment. We called the *Journal*, but they didn't want to fax it to us since that's not their policy. We didn't come up with the article. But, in the long run, the reporter was happy we didn't, because the *Journal* backed off the story within an hour: It wasn't true.

So, there's a danger in wanting to be real quick about things— if you're not sure and you're not being careful, you can make mistakes. One news organization might be embarrassed, but everybody who repeats it is embarrassed as well. So, our reporter was actually grateful that we didn't find the story.

Reading today's paper is not the end of the story anymore. Newspapers, NPR [130], CNN [34], Associated Press [18], are constantly updating their stories throughout the day on their Web pages. That's just one more way of getting to the information. We have reporters literally all over the world and only the one library here in Washington. So, I might send reporters an email message with links that they can click on and go right to a particular story, or a government site, or an organization, or a directory, or whatever, to see for themselves.

Even information from a reputable source may have changed the next time you see it.

Yes, or it may just be flat-out inaccurate. Remember, a year or two ago, on the floor of Congress, a representative from California got up to announce that Bob Hope had died? That came from the Associated Press. A lot of people don't realize it, but it is a fact of life in the news business; we work on obituaries in advance. Some reporter who should have been in his own private account was working on the Bob Hope obituary, and of course it had in the lead paragraph "XXX" for the actual date and time and place of his death, so any other journalist looking at that probably would have realized it wasn't an actual story. But somehow this story got onto the AP's Web page. A staffer in a congressional office saw it, didn't realize what it was, and immediately called to the floor, and it was announced. Then Bob Hope's daughter phoned the House of Representatives and said, "Excuse me, my father is not dead. I'm sitting across the table from him having breakfast." I don't want something like that to happen to NPR.

There certainly are times when we say, "We don't think you should use this information. We don't think this is valid. We can't find it in any reputable resource. A couple of different papers are reporting such and such, but it's not attributed. We can't find any primary source, or any organization or person directly involved in this who says it's true." We just have to give those cautions to the editors and reporters and let them make their decisions.

What do you find to be best and, on the other hand, most frustrating about the Internet?

One frustration is the delays. I don't have the fastest computer or a dedicated connection, but I'm not at the low end, either. We have, I think, made a good case at NPR that nobody needs faster computers than the library, and that whatever can be done to speed up our connectivity would be greatly appreciated. We frequently discuss with the IT department ways to improve the connection speed. But the Internet itself slows us down while it loads advertising, and I don't like that.

I use Switchboard [171] and the AT&T [13] directories quite a bit, but I almost always write down the phone number rather than print out the page because, with all the little graphics and things on it, it takes forever to send just that one piece of information to my printer. I'm hoping for a solution to these communication problems as soon as possible. The technical people have created this wonderful image of the online world; unfortunately, the reality isn't quite as good as it's presented. I'd like to see the reality come a little closer to the fantasy of instantaneous communication.

What's best? When everything is working well—quick access to primary material, the amazing number and variety of resources, access to kinds of information we didn't even dream of ten years ago, and the unlimited potential for the future.

What else would you like to see available online?

I'd like something that would allow me to search several commercial databases at once, plus maybe throw in a couple of Web search engines, and then show me a collection of results and let me select them and put them into a package that I can print or email to the user. I'm starting to see "consolidator" services, such as Webfeat.com [201], that can do that, and I think this is a very useful development.

Lexis-Nexis Universe is starting to add some actual reference books—*Encyclopedia of Associations*, some *Who's Who* directories, some other biographical tools. A small news library that has a serious budget problem, instead of buying some of these reference books, may be able to get them through Nexis, which is very advantageous. I hope to see more texts, reference books, and so on, available online.

Also, if I could communicate with all the Webmasters all over the world, I would ask them to think about the way their sites are used, and to provide basic information right there on their front pages. The number of university Web pages that do not provide an address and phone number is just astounding to me. I'd like Web sites to be easier to search and navigate, and I'd like to see some standardization of search protocols.

How do you keep and organize information from searches that you've done? Do you give

it to reporters in digital form, store it on your intranet, or do you hand it to them on pieces of paper?

We don't necessarily store the information we collect in answering queries. Anything I send by email stays in my Sent Items folder until I delete it. So if a reporter loses something, or if another person on the project needs the same information, I won't have to re-do the search. Sometimes, I'll print the results of a Web or database search, and add them to the clip file.

But we don't use our intranet to transmit or archive research. Our newsroom management software, ENPS [244] from the Associated Press, is a better place for that. For example, we put together a quick Yeltsin Fact Sheet the day he resigned, and stored it in the Foreign Desk's electronic folder where anyone can access it. ENPS is also where staff can find materials created for them by the librarians—Pronunciation Guide, Obits in Progress, Grammar Assistance, factsheets, etc.

How do you think news research might change in the next few years?

I think there will be more of everything—more Web sites, more advertising, more confusion, and more problems of authority, accuracy, and currency. But more information will be accessible more quickly, I hope, and that means more exciting challenges for us as we help each other sort it out! Reporters and librarians—or whatever we call ourselves—will be working even more closely together to provide our organizations with top quality research and reporting.

Super Searcher Power Tips

➤ One of the attractive features of Lexis-Nexis Universe is what they call "Personal News." You can read every newspaper in the world every single day for the topics you're following, or ask Nexis to do that for you.

➤ Stumpers is an international mailing list for difficult reference questions. Participants are from public libraries, for the most part, but it includes all kinds of interesting people worldwide. It's good for the kinds of resources that NPR doesn't have, that I know will likely be in a public library.

➤ In a flat-fee database, you don't worry about the clock ticking or costs mounting for every little modification. That's one of the reasons we let the reporters use flat-fee services; if the phone rings in the middle of their search, I don't want them to worry. Go ahead, take your phone call. Your search will still be there when you're done.

➤ I remind News staff that it's often a two- or three- or four-step process to come up with an answer to a question. Sometimes, a print source might be the best place to start.

➤ A small news library that has a serious budget problem, instead of buying some reference books, may be able to get them through Nexis, which is very advantageous.

C.B. Hayden

ABC News' Broadcast Research Leader

C.B. Hayden is Director of Research Services at the world headquarters of ABC News. He holds an M.L.S. degree from George Peabody College, Vanderbilt University. He speaks and writes frequently on issues related to the Internet, intranets within news organizations, and research journalism.

cb.hayden@abc.com
www.abc.com

Tell me a little about your background and how you got into news research.

Like many people, I've come to news research in a weird way. My undergraduate major was music. Very few people get into the news via music, but I'm always surprised by the number of people that I work with at ABC News who do not have a journalism background. I think a varied background is one of the best preparations for news research. I then studied music history and library science in graduate school at the Peabody College at Vanderbilt University in Nashville. While I was there, I took a job at a bank holding company that had just started a research department, and I was just sort of the "office kid." But I was the only one there who did a lot of research. That was at a time that many southern banks were investing heavily in foreign corporations, so I was doing a lot of that kind of research. I really liked it and seemed to have a talent for it. After I finished graduate school at Vanderbilt, I moved to New York City at the urging of a friend, and got a job at the Research Institute of America, which now is primarily a legal publisher. At that time, though, they had a number of different ventures going on, one of which involved doing in-depth business research for many of their subscribing clients. My boss there left to set up the first professionally staffed research department at ABC News. I quickly followed, and I've been here ever since.

You apparently had a real affinity for news research.

I guess so. I think having a business research background prepares you for almost anything. It certainly establishes strong problem-solving skills and thought processes. In a news organization, you're able to apply those skills to a much broader range of requests. We might handle just about anything here on a daily basis. So, my business background was good preparation for doing news research.

When I came to ABC, online information was just becoming widely available. There was no access to that type of information within ABC News other than *The New York Times* Information Bank, which was an abstract service that you could subscribe to. Nexis [106, see Appendix] had just become available. The day I walked in the door, I brought several other online systems with me, and we built from there.

I'm sure you've continued with a number of those traditional online services, but how did ABC make the transition into adding the Internet as a research component?

Actually, as I'm fond of bragging, the research center was the very first department within the entire corporation that had Internet access. We got interested in it after attending conferences. At that point, it was just a Unix prompt—no graphics or point-and-click. It was the Wild, Wild West. We learned as we went along, exercising our curiosity to find out what was out there beyond that daunting Unix prompt.

I remember the first time we were able to connect to the National Library of Indonesia, I think it was, via the Internet and check an Australian scientific paper that had somehow come up in a news story. We were able to use the Internet to trace information on the author. We were stunned by that power. I don't think any of us ever anticipated that—if you believe what you read in the newspapers and hear in other media—we would become practically an Internet-driven economy in just a few years. To us, it was just a great tool that provided access to many different computers worldwide that we had never had access to before. Now, there's not a single aspect of the work of the research center that the Internet hasn't revolutionized, altered, or had an impact on at some point.

Let's talk about how the research center functions with reporters. How closely do you work with journalists? Do you set up teams for particular projects?

We don't have teams. I'm blessed with a tremendous group of expert information professionals—or, to use the term we're beginning to use for ourselves, research journalists. We don't specialize in any way; we're all generalists. Among ourselves we know that some people have particular strengths and specialties, but we just take on all comers. Whoever picks up the phone speaks with a producer or a journalist. We work with all levels of ABC personnel. It's just as likely that an anchorperson will call us as an intern.

One of the aspects of our work, and perhaps the most difficult aspect of news research within a large news organization, is this information triage: How do we provide different levels of service? For some people, it doesn't matter what they ask for; we will try to find a logical answer for them, or find out why there *isn't* a logical answer. For others, we just have to tell them that they are not entitled to our service. Some people who come to work here have a difficult time adjusting away from that admirable tradition of altruistically providing research service to anyone who requests it. In a corporation, you just have to learn that that's not always the case.

We primarily talk to reporters on the phone and survey their needs—whether it's just a quick question, or an involved project. Because we put so much information out to the journalists' desktops via our intranet now, we ask that they do some of the work on their own, when appropriate. We try to help them do it, either by training or by talking them through it over the phone. We have had to move in that direction just because of the overwhelming demand for our services. In most news organizations, it's difficult to get more staff. So, encouraging end-user searching is a productivity technique, and necessary with our staffing.

In many cases, it's better for them to do it on their own. They come to the research with a different eye, a different set of skills and thought processes. That enables them to see something in a search that sets off bells for them that we as search intermediaries might not see. But the real goal is getting them to do some of the basic research on their own, so that we have added time to work on the more difficult and more costly projects, and to use resources to which they don't have access.

Do you provide formal training?

Yes, we do a tremendous amount of training. On average, I'd say we do two group sessions a week. That could be three people, or five or six in our own training room. For intranet training we've done sessions that had eighty people in them. We did two sessions for "20/20" with about eighty to a hundred people in each session; that was our one big theatrical performance. We did four large sessions in the Washington bureau. And this year we're doing an "Intranet World Tour," where Candace Stuart, our supervisor for online information services and our intranet coordinator, and I will split up our other bureau cities and do training sessions in all those bureaus. We do some over-the-phone training, too. Every day, all the information specialists work with journalists over the phone, showing them how to do searches and how to exploit the resources that they have access to for themselves.

What is on your intranet? What are you training them to use?

Our intranet has become the focus of our activity. On-demand research is still our biggest product. That's what the ten information specialists on the staff do all day long. Most of our resources still go to that on-demand research, but I suspect that the statistics for intranet use will very soon overshadow, if they don't already, the statistics for what we do on-demand. We're getting about 125,000 hits a month on our department's intranet site, and that's just from the news division.

The resources on the intranet are divided into two major categories. One consists of pages that we put together daily in response to breaking and on-going news. The other consists of more permanent pages related to specific subject areas. The breaking news pages are productivity tools for the journalists. They don't have to go out to a search engine and start plugging in keywords and hope that good stuff comes back. We evaluate, select, and organize sites and other resources and put them right there for them.

Give me an example of a breaking news story that you would work on.

Right now, the lead breaking news page—we call them Hot Link pages; I don't know who we stole that from, but I'm sure we didn't make it up—is the Middle East peace negotiations between Israel and Syria. So, we've got a whole section of background, with thirty or forty different resources on the page. Most of these are just links to free sites that journalists could find on their own if they had the time. But we feel that it's our role to save them that time. Even if they do know that those sites are out there, it's a convenience to not have to type in an address. All they have to do is click. We include government sites, think tanks that produce policy papers, various kinds of background information, links to maps. We include links to military profiles for each of the countries. We include biographical profiles for some of the major personalities involved.

You pull some of that from proprietary sources?

Yes. We subscribe to between fifty and seventy-five fee-based services that we provide over the intranet, many of which end users can search on their own, but many of which we can also link to directly for discrete information. We go to a site, find the information, and link directly to it. Again, it's a time-saver for the journalists. It lets them be more productive and more creative in their work. At least, that's the ultimate goal.

A page like that probably has thirty or forty different resources organized into subcategories. We try to design each page so journalists can quickly scan the page and start making decisions on what information is important to the piece they're working on and which of these resources would be best for them to use.

We also link out to other news media coverage of the issues. Say the BBC [22] has done a special report on the Middle East peace process, or Yahoo! [206] has done a whole page; we'll link to those kinds of things. We also link to ABCNews.com [4]. When we first started our intranet, we never linked to our own material. We just assumed that our users would go to ABCNews.com on their own, but through feedback we found that they really wanted us to link to our own material and pull in a lot of external material as well.

Putting together the Hot Link pages is something all the information specialists do daily. On a typical day, we probably put up between one and three new pages, and we maintain existing pages as well. So that's one focus of the intranet. The other aspect is our permanent subject categories. We maintain permanent pages for about thirty different subject categories. These are also a blend of external sites—free sites that we have evaluated and vetted and said, "Yes, these are the major ones you need to use if you're covering, for example, an air disaster"—along with links to those fee-based services that we subscribe to, as well as internal databases that the research center puts together.

In the past, we used to prepare these huge briefing books with background information. They were a technical nightmare to put together, but I think we led in doing that kind of proactive news research. Nobody ever asked us; we just took it upon ourselves to do them. They were wildly successful and dramatically changed how we were perceived within the news organization. Now we've translated all those skills into producing the intranet. But the intranet lets us pull together resources on a minute-to-minute basis, whereas in the past, a briefing book would take several weeks to produce. By the time we got it into the hands of reporters, it was still valuable but not nearly as up-to-date or complete as we'd like to have had it. We don't even produce printed versions anymore. The intranet gives us so much flexibility in presenting that kind of information. We go to the trouble of evaluating, reformatting, editing, and annotating information. I think that is one area that shows that our skills really are different from, and complementary to, those of the practicing journalist.

We still do some briefing books, but always an online version. It's either a PDF file or a Word file with a lot of material pulled together and reformatted, edited, and put together in a way that we think the journalists at ABC News will want to use it. For example, we have biographical profile packets on all the presidential candidates right now, and on most of their spouses, updated as needed. It keeps the whole intranet dynamic and current. It's easy to do and it's been a revolution for us.

What are your permanent subject categories? What kinds of things do you include?

We have a category for the major search services, the multipurpose online services available on the intranet, like DialogSelect [45], Dow Jones Interactive [48], ProQuest Direct [151], and Hoover's Online [85]. We have SIRS (Social Issues Resources Series) [164], Facts.com [61], which is the online version of *Facts on File* [229], the *Keesing's Record of World Events* [102], NewsBank NewsFile [134], Global NewsBank [78], some of the EBSCO [51] magazine databases, and a few others in that category. These are for people who are doing story idea development or just getting quick background information on stories that they're working on.

These are all available via everybody's desktop within ABC News, though it's primarily the editorial staff who are using them. We've worked with Dialog to develop a custom search interface that we think reflects how our journalists search and what's going to get the best information for them with the least amount of training on our part, and the least amount of search skill on the journalist's end. We've worked with a lot of online vendors to help develop custom interfaces for us.

How do the reporters handle a system like Dialog?

Reporters seem to have much more patience with bad search results than news researchers do. I want to do the best search ever and come up with the five best articles, but they're willing to sit and look at a couple hundred articles. Their patience for that, and the way their creative process works, seems to be a little bit different from ours. I think that they see value in getting a large search result back, but we see it as a waste of our time. I don't know who's right, but it seems to work for both of us. They do a really good job with it.

Of course, some people see searching Dialog and so on as "you're just trying to get us to do your work." They're in the minority, but we still are faced with that attitude. Then there are people who just jump in, and we seem never to hear from them again. They become almost *too* enamored of the resources we've given them. So the reaction varies.

All in all—and I think the statistics bear this out—all these services now on the intranet have been a hugely successful project for us, and one of which management is very supportive. I can brag that all these fee-based services that we've got on our intranet have not required a single budget increase. As you might imagine, management really likes that. And the end users have access to a universe of information that they never had access to before. I'm really seeing a difference in their attitudes toward information. Now that we've put this whole array of other sources on their desktops, they're starting to see that there's a lot more to news research than just doing a quick search of Lexis-Nexis, Dialog, or Dow Jones.

Let's go back to your intranet subject categories.

We have a category for Internet tools, where we list what we think are some of the best search engines. We have a page called Major News Sites, which provides quick access to some of the major online and Internet providers of news. We have a category called News Futures, which is where we put many in-house documents that serve as schedules of upcoming news events. We have Quick Info, which is a ready reference section. It includes a lot of free sources, but also some encyclopedias that we subscribe to.

We have Advance Obits, which are pages consisting of pre-pared biographical information on prominent people who, if they died, would generate huge news coverage. We've done eighty to a hundred pages so far that have links to various resources on a person's life. Those might include biographical profiles on a service such as Gale's Biography Resource Center [74], and a list of contact numbers for people associated with their lives—all the basic tools that somebody will need to cover the death of a prominent person. It's our responsibility to be for-ward-thinking and to be prepared.

As for actual subject categories on the intranet, the first one is air disasters; I won't go through all of them because we'd be here all day. What we tried to do with air disasters, as an example, is put together links to the basic information that someone needs to cover when a plane goes down. These include all the different FAA documents, all those databases of plane tail numbers, how to get graphics of a plane's livery, or how the planes are painted. How to get information on a specific aircraft, its specifications, its range, how many passengers, all the questions that we know go into the immediate coverage of an air disaster. Right now, that page is just listed like all of our other subject categories. But I'd really like to see it as a flow chart of how to do this kind of research—locate the tail number, then do this, or else do that—and make it a step-by-step process. So far, we haven't had the time to work on that. I'd really like to work on it with our in-house aircraft and airline industry experts.

We have a category for associations where we list not only Gale's Ready Reference Desk [75], which includes the *Encyclopedia of Associations*, but a number of other specialized association directories as well. There is a Biography category, which includes a lot of free biographical resources as well as the two we subscribe to, Gale's Biography Resource Center and Wilson Biographies Online [204].

We have a business and finance category, a campaign finance category, an education category, an entertainment and the arts category. We have an expert locator category, which lists a lot of different resources for quickly locating people who are experts in a particular field. We try to educate people that they need to use their most critical journalistic eye when dealing with any of the experts they locate in this way, just as they would with anybody they're speaking to as an expert on a story. But it is convenient for them to be able, in the middle of the night, to begin locating experts on a particular subject if a big story breaks.

We have an elaborate government and politics category, which includes many fee-based services. All of these categories, I think, include at least one fee-based service for value-added information that people can't just get for free off the Internet. We know the typical questions that we're going to get. If we see a trend in particular kinds of questions, we try to find a product that we can put on the intranet that can answer those questions. Every time we do that, we gain a lot of time back, and also make it easier for end users to take care of their own needs.

Do you ever hear reporters say that everything is on the Internet, they can get it all for free?

We used to be faced with a lot of that. Most of our people are a little more educated now. Journalists tend to be fairly savvy because of the curiosity factor. That's why many people become journalists. I think journalists were quick to understand that you get what you pay for on the Internet, and that, while there's a tremendous amount of wonderful information out there, people will charge money for some information because it has a lot of value.

It's the younger people I see who are more apt to want to trust solely stuff from the Internet. We have to educate them that there are other resources out there. The older journalists tend to be more Nexis-, Dialog-, and Dow Jones-oriented. They tend to ignore the Internet, and the younger people tend to ignore the fee-based services. So, another part of the educational process is to get them to understand the balance between the two kinds of information, and to make sure they're aware that, many times, they need to check both.

Another part of our educational process is to remind people about the entire universe of information locked in what you might call the most impregnable and difficult-to-search databases of all—hard-copy books, newspapers, and periodicals. Huge amounts of data are just not available electronically. People—journalists certainly—are doing themselves a disservice if they don't at least consider printed sources in covering a story.

When the same information is available in a number of places, how do you decide where to access it? Is cost a big factor?

Many times cost is a factor. But often, working on deadline or trying to meet demand, ease of access is something we're willing to pay for. I think some of the traditional online services have missed the boat by not making their data available in a much more easy-to-use format. If I can do a public records search on a Web-based system where you just fill in the forms and pull up records from a certain state, as opposed to having to use some Byzantine search language, I'm going to go with that fill-in-the-blank option every time. That's not to say that we don't understand that we need to have those other kinds of skills as well. Often, the in-depth searching that sets us apart is not something that you can do using those easy search interfaces. But if you're working under deadline, if you're under pressure to handle a lot of questions, sometimes you have to pay for that ease of access. Cost is always a factor but, many times, just getting the question answered quickly and authoritatively overrides that consideration.

When are the traditional online services still your best choice?

The traditional services do a better job of letting you do a comprehensive search across a wide range of databases very quickly. I also think they are beginning to do a very credible job of translating their services to the Web. Now, certainly in the case of Dow Jones, we don't use a dial-in interface. Many of my staff are beginning to make the transition to Lexis-Nexis Universe [107] just because it's convenient. It depends on the search. But that's what sets us apart from the journalists—we know how to evaluate information resources. We take a question and immediately say, "I'd better skip Lexis-Nexis Universe. I'd better use traditional Lexis-Nexis for this." Or, "There are five Dialog databases that I need to search for this. If I use traditional Dialog, I can search them all at once, dump out the duplicate records, and I'll have a good distillation of the results in just a few seconds."

And yet, if you let your journalists use Dialog Select and the others on their own, aren't they wasting a lot of time when you might be able to answer their questions in a few minutes?

They probably *are* wasting some time. But we urge them to call us if they have spent ten minutes on something and can't find what they want. Then, we'll begin the research interview process, trying to figure out why they didn't find it, what they can do to go back and quickly find it on their own—or, more likely, we say, "You're probably not going to find that there. You probably ought to call this person." Or, "Let me take a look and find two or three Web sites that might have this." Or, "Let me put you in touch with the correct person at XX." Or, "We just got a new book that has a chapter on that."

This information consulting work, which is a by-product of end-user searching, is a growth industry for us. The journalists don't feel that they're wasting their time, because they always find *something* they can use or something that's related to the search they're doing. But we stress in training that everything we offer the end user should be a time saver, not a time waster. We tell them, "Whenever you feel that your time is being wasted, you need to get on the phone to us, and we'll sort it out." The goal of our end-user searching system is never to waste their time. I would feel dreadful if I found that somebody was sitting for hours trying to find something and not complaining. But journalists are a very vociferous bunch. They are not shy about telling us when things are not working for them!

Let's talk about searching on the Net. It sounds as if you recommend that people not go directly to a search engine, but instead to a very specific page or recommendation on your intranet, which would then guide them to specific resources on the Net.

It depends. Certainly we try to get them to use our intranet, because we think that will be the best use of their time. But it's tough to break people of the habit of hopping over to Yahoo! or Go.com [79] or wherever, and just typing in keywords. It has taken a major educational effort to help them understand that a search engine doesn't really cover the entire universe of information, and that a lot of news research still involves looking at newspaper articles, magazine articles, and how someone else has covered a story. You get very little of that from search engines. Generally, they quickly see that you get a whole different type of information from search engines than you get from the more traditional database sources. Having access to all the Internet content that you get from search engines just gives us another way of looking at a story. I think we're fortunate that we have all the other resources as well, and they don't have to be dependent on search engines.

The amount of information on the Net has certainly grown dramatically. What can you find now that you just couldn't get a few years ago?

A major benefit is the immediacy of information on the Net—press releases that you would have had to call around for, or government information in the middle of the night. The government has really led industry and other types of organizations in strongly implementing Web access to a great deal of their information.

Every day, somebody comes up with a more creative way of presenting some new kind of information on the Net. Not too long ago, someone asked us for graphics of shark embryos. I can guarantee you that we do not have a book in our small collection that's going to have pictures of shark embryos. But, within five minutes, we had pictures of shark embryos that they were able to use for broadcast purposes. That kind of thing would have taken somebody hours and hours, if we'd even had that much time to invest. We probably would have had to tell them "start calling around" or "we really can't do this." Now, those kinds of things are so simple to do on the Net.

The only limitation now is your imagination. You can find a close approximation of what you're looking for in almost every case, or at least a lead to who might have it. I think the smart way to use the Internet is not to look for an answer, but to consider it a key that will open up something else. Even if we hadn't found those shark embryo graphics, we probably would have found a list of the major institutions that are doing shark research, and that would have immediately narrowed down our phone calling to two or three places. In the past, we might have had to make eight or ten calls to get to the right place. So, it's a big productivity boost for us, not only because end users can find a lot of the information they want, but also because it shortens the time that we have to spend researching the more difficult questions.

The Net has also changed the types of questions we're being asked. In the past, our research was pretty much text-based. But as more and more information becomes available in graphic format, and as more young people come into our organization who have grown up using information in graphic format, the nature of the questions is changing, and the type of research is changing to include information in graphic formats. Internet resources have led the change in the way information is presented.

What about electronic mailing lists or discussion groups? Do your researchers or journalists use them for contacts or background research?

Someone at "20/20" may come to me and say, for example, "We need to reach divorced mothers whose husbands have left the country." So, we could go to Usenet newsgroups and post messages and ask people to respond to an email address or call an 800 number. It puts producers in immediate contact with possible sources. Now, journalists and sources can interact directly for these people-related stories.

For a while, we did most of that for them, but now we're finding that our role is training them to do it on their own. One interesting finding is that a Usenet newsgroup may not be the best place to find sources, because those newsgroups still tend to attract mostly young people in college, and computer gearheads. We find that the commercial services, like AOL [10] or CompuServe [35], are sometimes better because you're more apt to reach a true "man on the street" or regular-type consumer.

Newsgroups and mailing lists can also be used when Web search engines just aren't current enough. I don't know of any search engine that is updated frequently enough to be useful for breaking stories. Often, though, if you search newsgroups, you can locate new Web sites relevant to stories long before those sites are ever picked up by a search engine. During our initial coverage of the school shooting incident in Littleton, Colorado, we searched newsgroups and were able to locate Web sites that had been set up that day. Newgroups can provide an immediacy that search engines often cannot.

In addition, we redistribute in-house about twenty-five or thirty different news services that we get via email. I urge other news organizations to go out and look for these things, because not only have they brought a constant stream of story ideas to our producers, but they have set us librarians apart as the people who know where to go to find this information. We are pushing these story ideas out to our people.

For example, we subscribe to one called Sports Business Daily [223], which is a daily news service covering the sports indus-try—I call it the "sports-industrial complex." There are a tremen-dous number of stories that you don't see in a daily newspaper's sports coverage, which generally focuses on events and person-alities. But, this news service covers the industrial and business underpinnings of professional sports.

We get another called China News Digest [213], which is a daily summary of news from within China. As our relationship with China changes and becomes more complex, it's really good to be forwarding this to our people who are charged with cover-ing China on a daily basis. It's a constant stream of specialized news. We get a number of others, such as one on Iran and several on Russia and the former Soviet Union.

The Internet has made access to these very specialized and niche news resources available at our fingertips, and this kind of specialized news is exactly what journalists need. Most newspa-pers, magazines, and television and radio news programs report consumer news rather than the highly specialized news that a journalist needs, and that in the past had to be gathered in various manual ways. A lot of that can now be automated. Finding these news services and redistributing them to our users has become a nice niche industry for us that requires very little work on our part. But we get a lot of benefit from it because we're seen as the people who know how to do it.

What about your personal preferences for using the Net? Do you use broad search engines? Metasearch engines? Very specific sites?

I'm just a prostitute, I guess, as far as search engines are concerned, because I change all the time. I get good results with HotBot [86] one day, so I'll use HotBot for two weeks. Then I'll *not* get such good results, and I'll try another search engine. I'll go to Go.com and get really good results, so I'll stick with them for a while. For several weeks now, I've been Google-mad. It seems that, with Google [80], no matter what search I put in, the first two or three hits that come up almost always take care of the question for me.

If you ask me this question next week, some other fantastic search engine probably will have supplanted Google; right now, though, I'm a real Google fan. But I think it's good for people to switch around. If I see somebody using Yahoo! constantly, I will suggest using something else for a while.

One of the best pieces of advice I ever got—I think that Nora Paul said this; it sounds so much like her—was to decide on one search engine and learn everything you can about that search engine so you can really do those in-depth, complex kinds of searches. Don't exclude the other ones, but have one that you really are knowledgeable about. In the research center, we'll pick several major search engines. Each person on the staff is responsible for having in-depth knowledge of a particular one. If a question comes up, we can discuss it among ourselves and decide which search engine might produce better results.

I think most of us switch around like that. On the portion of the intranet where we list the search engines, we juggle them around every once in a while, just so people don't get in the habit of picking the first one on the list. Whatever we group at the top of the page gets used a lot more than what's at the bottom, so we pay attention to how we list things.

How do you stay updated on everything you need to know about the online services as well as what's happening on the Internet?

Like most everybody else, I suspect, I wish I had several more hours a week to spend on that. I subscribe to quite a few email newsletters that describe new resources, new search techniques, that kind of thing. I subscribe to updating services from some of the search engines. One source that I use religiously, and insist that the staff pay careful attention to, is the Scout Report [220]. Many services out there announce new Internet resources, but the Scout Report does such a good job of editing them down. It seems that a large proportion of the resources they list every week have some news application, even in the scientific and engineering Scout Report. I'm amazed how often those are useful for news research.

That's not to say that I totally ignore print resources. I look at almost all the major computer magazines; at least I scan their table of contents every issue. I also check titles like *Yahoo! Internet Life* [243], which is a consumer view of Internet techniques and resources. They're important to pay attention to, because those are the kinds of resources that your end users are going to come back to you with, rather than some super-technical thing that you read about in the Scout Report. They're going to read something in the Yahoo! magazine about how you find good movie reviews, and that's going to be their knowledge base. I think it's particularly important that you keep in mind what your end users are going to know about the Internet.

We do a lot of talking among ourselves, which is probably the most valuable thing that we do to stay current. If people find some new resource that does the trick for them, it's part of the teamwork among staff and researchers to make sure that everybody else knows about it. There's an awful lot of email going back and forth among us. One example is about using ProQuest, one of our fee-based services. I had been emailing individual articles I'd selected back to myself. It had never occurred to me that there was a button you click on that lists *all* the articles you've selected and emails them all at once. It was a big breakthrough to discover that. Over the course of a year, it will save me four or five hours, so it's not a minor thing to discover those little tips. I wanted to save everybody else some time by cluing them in on it. To my surprise—because they are generally much more advanced searchers than I am—they didn't know about it. For once, I was the guy who knew something nobody else knew.

What do you like best about what you do?

It's just my personal nature to be very curious about everything. And, to be honest, I don't have a very long attention span. In news research, everything changes every day, every minute. You never know, when you pick up the phone, what you're going to be faced with. So, the constant turnover of different types of requests is appealing to me.

I really like to get positive feedback from our users. In broadcast news, and certainly within our organization, you very rarely get a lot of lavish praise; it's just not the nature of the business. Everybody's busy, and you don't get constant positive feedback from people, but when you *do*, you know you've really done a good job. We always just assume we've done a good job if we don't hear something negative. When somebody does take the time out of a very busy day to say that you or someone on your staff did a really good job that turned around the way they were looking at a story, or had some tremendous positive impact on the story, that is very gratifying.

It's also gratifying, and scary at the same time, to pick up the phone, give somebody a very quick answer, and literally thirty seconds later hear it come out of Peter Jennings' mouth. It's scary, and it's a big responsibility, because you're speaking for not only the entire news organization but ultimately the entire corporation when you do that.

Not long after coming to work at ABC News, Melinda Carlson, who runs our Washington Bureau Research Center, found herself sitting in the shadows of a television studio with an earpiece while Ted Koppel covered President Nixon's funeral. While the rest of the research team had prepared background material for his live, on-air coverage of the funeral, it fell to Melinda to be the one in the studio listening to Ted talk and making the decisions on what information to pass along to him and his producer. Melinda calls it her trial by fire!

All those stressful situations, where we are under a lot of pressure to be not only fast but also accurate, while not very pleasant when they are happening, always contribute to making us better equipped intellectually and emotionally to handle the next situation. It's one thing to be a good searcher and another thing entirely to be a good searcher when you have seconds to locate specific information, verify its accuracy, and emotionally mute the producer who is yelling in your ear!

Breaking news, such as an air disaster, almost always leads to instances of research results going directly from our hands to viewers. When John F. Kennedy Jr.'s plane crashed, the Research Center was instrumental in feeding information to Lisa Stark, ABC's transportation correspondent, and her on-location producers. Searches on DBT Online [41] for information on the history of the plane, and phone calls to the Coast Guard for ocean depths, yielded information that went almost instantaneously from the researchers' hands to the television viewers' eyes and ears.

Looking ahead a bit, how do you think research and reporting methods might change over the next few years?

I see us not working together in the research center. I see us out in the newsroom and at the different production units. Certainly, if we shift even more to end-user searching, our role will change to that of coach, trainer, hand-holder. We're already doing quite a bit of that, but I think that in five years there may not even *be* a research center. Our physical collection of research materials could be moved somewhere else. We'll just be in contact through various electronic methods. Probably somebody will manage whatever's left of that collection and the rest of us will be scattered among the different buildings, doing work at the various production units all day long, and maybe getting together once or twice a day to hash things over and plot out a strategy for the rest of the day.

I see us becoming wandering consultants within the next five years or so, if it even takes that long. It's something that I'm actually looking forward to, because I think we'll get credit for our full value when people see us sitting at their desks with them, getting them directly to the information that they want, rather than trying to talk them through it over the phone. We'll be at their meetings and contributing, and that's going to be good for the whole news organization.

Information management and research needs to be integrated throughout the entire production process, rather than just supporting background research and fact-checking. These information gathering and information management skills are what we need to bring directly to the production units. We can help them establish databases related to a particular story, where they can organize their notes, background research, Web sites, experts, interview transcripts, all that kind of stuff. It's sort of a litigation support system for journalists; it would be a reportage support system instead. I think that's where we're going. It's unavoidable if we want to remain viable. It's certainly not something we're resisting. We'd like to do it right now.

Frankly, I think the best thing that will ever happen to us is to get away from our association with the *book*. People walk into a room, they see some books on shelves, and they immediately have a preconceived idea of what you are and what you do. That often limits the way they react to you and interact with you. I am a huge fan of exploiting a well-developed and well-edited collection of print materials, but I don't think our users understand that the bulk of what we do for them now is totally unrelated to that kind of resource. We have one of the best print collections in the entire news industry. I don't want to get rid of the collection. I just don't want people to *see* it!

Where we need to head is toward managing and fully exploiting information in *all* its formats. Our future lies in providing better research service to our users and, ultimately, making a much more valuable—and *valued*—contribution to the production of better and more competitive reportage.

Super Searcher Power Tips

➤ We subscribe to between fifty and seventy-five fee-based services that we provide over the intranet, many of which end users can search on their own, but many of which we can also link to directly for discrete information. It's a time-saver for the journalists. It lets them be more productive and more creative in their work.

➤ I'm starting to see a difference in reporters' attitudes toward information. Now that we've put this whole array of other sources on their desktops, they're starting to see that there's a lot more to news research than just doing a quick search of Lexis-Nexis, Dialog, or Dow Jones.

➤ I still think the traditional services do a better job of letting you do a comprehensive search across a wide range of databases very quickly. I also think that they are beginning to do a very credible job of translating their services to the Web.

➤ The smart way to use the Internet is not to look for an answer, but to consider it a key that's going to open up something else to you.

➤ Newsgroups and mailing lists can be used when Web search engines just aren't current enough. I don't know of any search engine that is updated frequently enough to be useful for breaking stories.

➤ We redistribute twenty-five or thirty different email news services in-house. The Internet has made access to these very specialized and niche news resources available at our fingertips, and this kind of specialized news is exactly what journalists need. Most newspapers, magazines, and television and radio news programs report consumer news rather than the highly specialized news that a journalist needs.

➤ Decide on one search engine and learn everything you can about that one so you can do in-depth, complex kinds of searches. Don't exclude using other search engines, but have one that you really are knowledgeable about.

➤ Many services announce new Internet resources, but the Scout Report does such a good job of editing them down. A large proportion of the resources they list every week have some news application, even in the scientific and engineering Scout Report.

Annabel Colley

The BBC's Leading Investigative Broadcast Researcher

Annabel Colley is currently on an internal BBC assignment to a pilot Knowledge Management initiative called the BBC Programme Makers Workbench Project. She spent six years at BBC Panorama—the world's longest-running investigative documentary program—first as information researcher on the team, then as the Panorama Web site producer. She holds an M.Lib., is Chair of the Association of U.K. Media Librarians, and is a published author and speaker on computer-assisted research and reporting in the U.K. and Europe.

annabel.colley@bbc.co.uk
www.bbc.co.uk

Tell me about your background and how you came to do research for the BBC.

I was trained as a librarian and sort of fell into media librarianship. After graduating from library school, I worked in the library of London Weekend Television and, after only a short period, I was hooked. I joined the BBC as a film librarian in the Film and TV Library almost eleven years ago, and then moved to the press-cutting library at the BBC, where I worked for about four years. Most researchers in television and radio in the U.K. do not have a library background. They tend to be people with lots of journalistic contacts and ideas—journalists on the first rung of the ladder. As both a librarian and researcher, I am the exception rather than the rule. It is quite difficult for librarians at the BBC, and indeed at newspapers in the U.K., to move into program research; that is, to actually work on programs, such as Panorama or news bulletins, or to work very closely with journalists.

However, in the late 1980s, there was a move toward attachment systems, in which librarians from the press-cutting library would go and work on production teams. That is how I did it. We are called information researchers. There are four or five of us assigned to different current affairs programs in the BBC. We were originally just there on attachment, but we became so valuable on the production team that we actually became employed by the programs. Basically, we act as middlemen between the production teams that we work with and both external information sources and the internal BBC libraries. Our role is accessing books, cuttings, databases, and different sources of information. We are not actually based in the library.

What kinds of research do you get to do?

I was the information researcher at BBC Panorama between 1994 and 1999, and then the Web site producer for Panorama [23, see Appendix], which is quite a different job. But most of my experience is with online research, and that's what I'll talk about. I still write and lecture on the subject. Panorama is the world's longest-running current affairs documentary series; it started in May 1953. Panorama is an investigative program that is considered the flagship for current affairs investigative programs at the BBC.

Because of the nature of investigative journalism, the research basically never stops. The difference between traditional journalism and investigative journalism is the time spent. Every single contact, every expert, every angle, every document, every book is looked at initially, and so research involves accessing a wide range of material for producers. There are about forty producers, assistant producers, and reporters on the team so, on any one day, I could be looking at nine or ten different subjects. Or I might spend the whole day just working on one subject in depth.

It takes about seven weeks to put a typical Panorama program together. But there are many atypical programs. One type is what we call "access" programs, which depend on access to individuals or institutions. For example, we did a program on two British nurses who were being held in a Saudi Arabian prison for the murder of a colleague. Through the skill and contacts of our reporter, we gained access to the letters between the nurses and their families at home. That's what we call access programming, where we actually get access to a good contact that the reporter has.

We do many social affairs documentaries; we'll look at the future of the family, at parenting, at welfare crises. We also do the big international stories, which don't tend to get the large audiences that the social affairs documentary-style programs get. But as the world's largest public-service broadcaster, we have earned the right to do the big expensive programs, like the specials on Kosovo, by doing the more populist social programs.

So, with some exceptions, a typical program takes seven weeks—say, three weeks research, two weeks filming, and then another two weeks editing. But some programs might take a year to make if they depend on access to a prison, or a government department, or something like that. It can be very pressured, because I'm working for the whole team. I'm not just working on one program at any one time. The entire time one program is in production, four or five others are also rolling along in production.

On top of that, all the other producers will be coming to me for forward planning and ideas. The percentage of research material that actually makes it to the screen in a major investigation is quite small. Lines of inquiry have to be pursued in order to be dismissed, and negative checks have to be made. In a daily deadline newsroom, a lot of forward planning has to do with news pegs, wires, press releases, and lists of forthcoming events. We can't rely on future events lists or even press releases. Once news has made it into a press release or into the public domain, it could be considered old news for us. Forward planning and generating ideas in investigative journalism is more of a time-consuming intelligence operation.

Journalists are always coming to me with broad topics and subjects, and that's where the Internet is quite useful. Sometimes, you've just got a really broad approach to a subject, and you need to get a feel for what's out there. Then it gets honed down and down, so you're juggling lots of different angles.

When you start with a broad topic on the Internet, is there a general approach or method that you follow? Give me an example of what you might do.

Yes. If I had a very broad subject, and wanted to do a global, comprehensive search but wasn't sure what I wanted or what the best terms were, I would probably use a Web directory like Yahoo! [206]. Or I might do a search on AltaVista Advanced [8] or another general search engine, although I personally find the general search engines a lot less helpful.

I would combine Web searches with commercial databases. I am a massive user of Lexis-Nexis [106] and FT Profile [73], though I use Lexis-Nexis more at the moment. I would start very broad in my search, but I wouldn't be so concerned with sorting the material until I had honed it down to what I wanted. At this point, I would just want to see what is out there. Someone might ask about the subject of deep ecology, for instance, which I knew nothing about, and still don't know an awful lot about. But just putting in abstract terms on the Internet is quite useful, because it can give you a great start at that brainstorming stage.

What would you do after that?

Although I start broad, I would never look at more than about thirty hits. If I got more than thirty hits on AltaVista, I would go back and reformulate my search. I might use domain searching, like *title:environment* or *domain:gov*, for example. You can do this in AltaVista Advanced. I always tell people, when I'm training them, even if you don't think you're an advanced searcher, use the advanced search capability, because it gives you more power and control over the way you search. It allows you to find just reliable government sites, or sites registered in the U.K., or, in the case of my "title" example, the word "environment" occurring in the title, which usually means more relevance that just a passing mention anywhere on a Web page. I would also use all the Boolean operators; that's where the librarian training comes in.

Then I'd go down the list of results and look, first and foremost, at the sources. I'd go for the U.K.-oriented ones, assuming it's a U.K. subject, first, and for the academic institutions and government departments, and the news organizations or other recognized organizations that I can trust.

Getting the news on Yahoo! is great for the general public to just get a feel for the headlines, but it's not really news from a trusted, traditional source. I'd much rather look at the news organizations and say, "right, that comes from the BBC [22], from Reuters [159], from *The London Times* [110] or the *Telegraph* [39]"—the traditional organizations that I associate with a history of solid journalism. Some of the newer sources, I feel, don't have any real journalism in them. All they're doing is rehashing the wire copy out there on the Internet. That's okay if you want quick fact-checks, but if you want deep analysis and proper journalism, then go for the classic news organizations.

For government press releases, I would go to the individual U.K. government departments to actually search their press releases. There's also a U.K. government departmental site, the Central Office of Information [179], where you can actually search organized press releases. I find that very useful for seeing what a minister has said about a certain topic.

What guidelines do you have for going to a traditional service versus using the Net?

Three or four years ago, I was using the Internet just for the quirky stuff, the offbeat information, and relying on traditional sources, the commercial databases, for the rest. Now, the distinction is really blurring, because a lot of the commercial databases are moving to Web front-ends. However, as long as full-text news services like Lexis-Nexis exist, I would always use them first for old newspaper articles, particularly anything older than about a month, and particularly when I'm on a deadline. The simple fact is that you can cross-file search the archives of thousands of news sources at once. The archives go back 30 years in some cases. You are paying for highly organized, fast access to archives. The Web is great for looking at today's *London Times* if you live in Australia, but if you want older material, it is not the best place to go because it is too hit-or-miss and time-consuming.

I don't use the Internet for news wires since, at the BBC, like most news organizations, we have our own computer system that is infinitely faster and more reliable, and we have all the wires coming in from around the world.

The Net, however, is more exciting in terms of pictures, which can give you insight into a story. It can also provide ideas, tips, potential program contributors, and angles not found in the mainstream press, especially via mailing lists and newsgroups.

Let's talk about the traditional online services moving to Web versions. For example, the *Financial Times* now is putting all their effort into FT.com [66]. Have you found that the Web-based systems have compromised capabilities or power?

No, I think they're really getting there now. I have to admit it; I don't think they are compromised at all. I think the functionality is there. To begin with, I had accounts with both traditional dial-up access to Lexis-Nexis and Lexis-Nexis on the Web, because the problem I'd found was that there weren't as many sources on the Web version. But that's changed. We were using a Web-based service called Nexis ReQUESTer, which had just 5,000 sources compared with the half-million or so sources available through the dial-up service. But Lexis-Nexis Universe [107], which was rolled out in Europe in the last year, has almost the same number of sources as the dial-up service. Since we started using the Web version almost exclusively, our bills on Lexis-Nexis have fallen quite steeply.

Besides the traditional services now available through the Web, what resources are you now finding on the Internet that you couldn't get access to a few years ago?

I started using the Internet in about '95, and it was so different from the way it is now. With all due respect, it was ninety-nine percent American—which was great if I needed American material, but not so good for domestic content. I was also using it a lot for United Nations and other major international organizations' Web sites. Now, there are many more U.K. search engines, like U.K. Plus [182] and our BBC news online service, which is a great source for story background, with an archive back to 1997.

Back in '95, access to information on our own government here in the U.K. was almost nonexistent. However, the sources that I'm finding invaluable now are official U.K. government department sites, like HMSO (Her Majesty's Stationery Office) [85], where you can obtain U.K. government publications. The HMSO site has all public acts going back to 1996, and bills, and white papers, and research reports. This has been absolutely incredible, because it saves us money and time on sending out couriers on dispatch bikes, and that's a real boon.

One problem, though, is the degree of access to government information and personal data compared to what American journalists have available. There's a huge gap between what is possible in the States and what we can do here because of our data protection, privacy, and freedom of information laws. We can't get access in the same way that U.S. journalists can; I know that from IRE [99] (Investigative Reporters and Editors) seminars I have been to. Of course, it is not as simple as some British journalists might think it is, but your legislation means that you have access in a way that's just impossible here.

For example, do you have access to driving records, home ownership, or voter registrations?

No, absolutely nothing. The big breakthrough is that we've just gotten the U.K. Electoral Roll On-Line, via a commercial database service called Cameo [29]. I used to use a service for reverse number searching that worked about sixty percent of the time. It was a CD-ROM called InfoDisk, but we now use a site called 192.com [2]. However, the facility for reverse number searching of U.K. numbers was removed under our data protection laws. We are up against data protection all the time. It's a double-edged sword, because most people here would find it extremely uncomfortable to be able to find out everything about individuals the way you can in the U.S. But we are used to working within our laws.

On a personal level, however, I am very interested in keeping up with what is going on in computer-assisted research and reporting (CARR) worldwide. I just find it fascinating.

CARR is such a good concept and such a good way to sell the skills of information professionals. For the talks I give, I interpret CARR in the widest sense, as journalism using electronic sources. I show reporters some examples of what has been done, particularly from certain U.S. newspapers. I say, "I know we can't do it in quite this way yet, but I have managed to do a little CARR here at Panorama." I then show them other ways of using the Internet and online sources for research.

I have several examples of how I have used U.S.-style CARR on Panorama to assist on stories, in particular how I got access to a child homicide database held by a U.K. police department, in order to back up the central point of a film we were making in 1995 on pedophiles. In another example, I show how I used data on the carbon lobby in the U.S. to back up a 1997 program on the effects of the lobby on the worldwide negotiations to cut CO_2 emissions. I got to this data by searching a database from Environmental Working Group [55].

How do you deal with the integrity and authority of material found on the Net? What do you advise your reporters?

At the BBC, we have rigorous legal and editorial guidelines. At Panorama, we are so used to checking and double-checking every single source that we automatically mistrust nearly everything. Over the years we have dealt with just about every legal and editorial issue you could imagine. We are so careful. Checking all information is intrinsic among the most experienced. I tell the more junior and less experienced researchers outside Panorama that I teach to apply exactly the same criteria that librarians would apply to assessing a reference book: currency, accuracy, quality, objectivity.

Another thing I teach is to use the communication power of the Internet. Email the people who created the Web page, and if they are the people you think they are, they're going to become a good source for you. This is exactly what happened when I found a site called the Penal Lexicon [143], which is basically a prison and crime portal with a U.K. slant. It has loads of resources, all sorts of prison and crime information for the U.K, and all the government inspection reports, including maps of the layouts. I teach people how to identify bits within URLs—"gov," "edu," and so on—although even that can fail, because people can register bogus domains. I could see this prison site wasn't a government site, so I automatically mistrusted it. If you mistrust a source, I say email the person who set the Web page up and be quite blunt about it: "Why did you set the page up? Who's funding you? How often do you update the site?" I mention that I'm a BBC journalist and why I need to know this sort of information. On this occasion, the person who set up the prison page was an ex-Home Office researcher. The Home Office is the government department that deals with crime and domestic affairs. He became a useful contact.

What about using mailing lists or similar sources for people contacts and information gathering?

Lists are one of the most useful resources for me. When I first started using the Internet, it was all searching the World Wide Web and building up my bookmarks. Now, in order to stay on top of what sources are out there and what's new, I hardly ever search the Web. I rely on mailing lists. One mailing list I'm a member of is NewsLib [222], the American SLA (Special Libraries Association) News Librarians mailing list, which I get in digest form. What's so useful about it is that it's a community of users, and I personally know some of the people. I can put out a request for information and I know that someone will help me.

The Association of U.K. Media Librarians [19], of which I am chair, is the equivalent organization to the SLA News Division, although we're much smaller. We have our own listserv, which is growing, and we exchange information about new sites and anything else of interest to media librarians working in broadcasting, newspapers, and magazines.

Probably the most useful email newsletter source in the U.K. for online and Internet research tips is a source called Free Pint [72], as in going into a pub and getting a free pint! It has a quirky brand, and people quite like that. It has almost 30,000 subscribers to its email newsletter. There's an element within it called the Free Pint Bar, which is a forum where you can get all sorts of tips. I wrote a piece on computer-assisted journalism for the site. Authors, usually information professionals, write articles that appear every two weeks, and it's absolutely invaluable for hearing about really good sources.

I also use "ResearchBuzz" by Tara Calishain [219], and one from UKOLUG, the U.K. Online User Group [181]. That gives me lots of tips about new ways of searching and new Web sites, and it keeps me on top of current issues in the online information world.

To find people for programs, I use ExpertNet [60] to find U.K. academics. I also use Mailbase [114] to locate high-quality U.K.

academic mailing lists. This enables you to search online archives in an incredibly sophisticated way before deciding whether to join a list. I currently recommend using RemarQ [156] to search the archives of newsgroups to find potential story ideas, offbeat and grass roots discussions of a new disease or drug, or to locate someone who has experienced an event. I find Deja.com [42] has become confusing for searching newsgroups. It's too much of a portal now; it's trying to do too much.

Do you have an example of a favorite news research project or one that was particularly challenging?

I worked on a program called "Kosovo, the Reckoning." I mentioned earlier that a program normally takes seven weeks to make. There are exceptions. "Kosovo, the Reckoning" went out in June '99, and basically charted the road to the peace deal in Kosovo. This is what we would call a "fast-turnaround" program. Most Panoramas are single-topic forty-minute films, but studio-produced films or a mixture of studio and other short films, all in the forty-minute range, are used for this fast reactive programming. When an event like this happens, we have to work like a daily newsroom, and we have a deadline of maybe seventy-two hours to put a program together. But, because of who we are and what we're expected to do, we still have to do all the in-depth investigations with all the different elements. So, "Kosovo, the Reckoning" was a typical fast-turnaround program where it's "all hands on deck." We all worked literally day and night over a weekend.

Other examples of reactive programs were when the Princess of Wales died, and when there's an IRA bombing. When that happens, everyone turns to us to deliver the definitive program. Everyone's done all the news stories, they've done all the different news angles, and at the end of the day, or the end of the week, they turn to Panorama to provide the final analysis or tell them something new. That's the pressure that's on us—to give the final word.

With the Kosovo program, we looked at many different elements. We had a studio debate with key military strategists giving their opinions on the peace negotiations. We had three different film packages, one of which was called "The Road Back Home," in which one of our reporters went out and spent time with the refugees and reported back. Then we had a piece from the States where another reporter went out and talked about the negotiations, and another piece from Serbia, from the actual bombing area.

I don't know how I ever managed without the Internet for programs like this. Before, I would photocopy masses and masses of hard copy press cuttings from the library, with all the different little angles that we might need for this program. For example, for the bit in the studio where we had the military strategists talking, I would find quotes and analysis, "think pieces," academic essays, and so on, as well as people who had different, conflicting opinions to participate in the debate. What's really great now is that a source like BBC News Online, or any of the big news sites like CNN [34], or an organization like the Institute for War and Peace Reporting [96], will have Kosovo special pages. They'll have the key players, and they'll have biography and background for key figures, as well as chronologies, timelines, angles, and issues. Those are great places to start. But the Web sites don't always have the real in-depth quotes, just the surface news. Some opinions will have appeared only in the military, strategic, or defense journals.

Do you use Lexis-Nexis for something like that?

Yes, I used Lexis-Nexis for sources like *Aviation Week* and *Defense News*. I might have been able to track those publications down on the Internet, but the chances of their having archives available, and the time I would have wasted trying to find them, would not have been worth it. I knew they'd be there on Lexis-Nexis, and I knew I could get them in minutes, and time is of the essence when facing a seventy-two-hour turnaround.

We had to choose two military strategists, from about twenty, to appear in the studio. We also had an interview with the Prime Minister. David Dimbleby, who is our key reporter and presenter for programs like this, obviously needed the backup research to prepare all the background. He likes lots and lots of really well-written briefs for his political interviews, so those all had to be written, as well. Everything Tony Blair's ever said on every angle, on every aspect of the war, of the bombing campaign, of the military strategy, of NATO, opinions on different people—all those quotes I sourced from Lexis-Nexis and from some Internet news sites.

It's a really difficult task for the information researcher, because we may go through twenty different key figures to find the one or two who are actually going to make it to the screen. The journalists have to know what that person's been saying, know what their exact opinion is on strategy, so that they can phone them up and try to get them on the show. And they have to appear well informed, even if they've had to consolidate all this information incredibly quickly. So, a lot of our work is getting all the quotes, actually tracking them down, writing a brief, and consolidating all the information for the assistant producers to use their powers of persuasion in getting people on the show.

Because he was interviewing the Prime Minister, the reporter obviously had to know what the Foreign Minister had been saying, so I went to the Ministry of Defence Web site [180], where they have all their press releases, and the NATO site [131] for policy statements and running daily press briefings. I also covered some human rights watch sites to get all the angles on the refugees, because one of our reporters wanted to track down families in Kosovo and talk to them, and to interview heads of aid agencies like Médicins Sans Frontières.

In what form do you collect all this information and present it? Do you put it all on an intranet? Do you send files electronically by email, or hand people paper copies?

I use a mixture of electronic and paper methods. I also do desktop shortcuts by just right-hand mouse-clicking on any Web page in my browser. This creates a shortcut directly to the Web site from the desktop. I also email highly selected favorites to people. But reporters still want it on paper in front of them in order to start calling people on the phone. When we worked with press cuttings, they were literally photocopied packages, with about ten copies of every cutting for each angle of research—one for the reporter that was going abroad, and one for the producer that was perhaps also going on location, and the researcher that was based in the office would also want one. Then, as the work increased, another researcher or additional producers would be brought in at a later stage, and they would want copies of the same material. Fast-turnaround programs might involve ten people. I would joke that it was like a primary school nature or science topic table, with lots of labels and samples on top of every available cupboard and filing cabinet in the office. When it was a fast-turnaround program, I just cleared the decks and labeled everything so that everybody had all the different angles, and people could then come along and take a package of material.

When we first did these Panorama programs, a mass of material and a mass of work went into them, so we tried to keep all the paper material. But because there's so much material and so many different angles, we ended up not doing that.

I'm sure you track some of these topics multiple times. How do you keep track of what you've done previously so that you don't have to repeat your research?

What I have done and haven't done is usually in my head, and everything is written down in my red book. Everyone researching at the BBC carries a red book! I am so totally focused that I think of nothing else. Your adrenaline keeps you going.

When we did the Kosovo program, I knew that there would probably be another two or three Panorama programs on Kosovo over the next few months. So we kept all the Internet sites, first just as shortcuts on the desktop, and then I'd put them all into categorized bookmarks or favorites. Then we could go back to access those bookmarks for other programs.

Are your bookmarks accessible to multiple people over the network?

Not yet. Things are moving in that direction in various ways, but people just aren't quite ready to have everything one-hundred-percent electronic. It's a major consideration when we do a fast turnaround on an international program; the reporter needs a hard copy in his hand because there's so little time that they have to take that and literally get up to speed in the taxi or the plane on the way to the interview. Although it's the future, we're not yet in a position to be totally electronic. I'd love to just email all the bookmarks to the hotel where the reporters or producers are staying, so they could access them on a laptop. Infrastructure costs are a consideration, though, as well as techno-fear.

We do have a system that enables people to log in to the internal BBC network from remote places, but it's quite expensive for programs to pay BBC computer support guys to do that for large numbers of people on the current system. Only editors and very senior reporters tend to be able to do it, at the moment.

However, to encourage the staff to move forward, I prepared laminated tip sheets, including one called "Guide to Internet and intranet sources for Panorama journalists on the road." What I've done is very much like Nora Paul's idea—list the tasks they're trying to do on the left side of a chart, and put the URLs on the right side, with notes about their features. I tell them, if you can access the Internet at home—or from a laptop in a hotel or a cybercafe or wherever you happen to be—the sources in one color are the Internet ones; the sources in another color are the ones on the BBC intranet if you can dial into the internal network. I know that some people use them; I still see them floating around the office on people's desks. But the liability of being an information researcher on a program is that they know you're there to do the work for them, so they will keep calling you to do it for them. I am a victim of my own success, really!

To try to make my life and the life of my colleagues easier, I built an intranet site called "Using the Internet for Research." I wanted colleagues at Panorama to be able to go to one centralized place instead of trawling through old emails hunting for the favorites embedded in them. Ironically, the people on my own program used it the least because they knew I was there to do research for them! But it has been a much bigger success story in pushing computer-assisted research at the BBC generally. I marketed it at some lunchtime demos and it became tremendously popular among factual program makers all over the BBC.

Again, it listed tasks like finding experts and contacts, ideas, facts, and so on, and then led them to direct Web sources, all in clear charts. It's a way to filter the overload of the Internet. I did the intranet site, using the already-existing huge BBC intranet infrastructure, in my own spare time. But I didn't have the time to update or maintain it, so I took the idea and the task-based approach to the head of the BBC Information and Archives directive (the BBC Libraries department). The BBC libraries are a massive operation with 500 librarians and support staff in the London libraries and almost 200 staff in the U.K. regions. I put the idea to him, and it got funding, and I was involved in a major computer-assisted research project as consultant.

The project, called "Research Central," will relaunch the existing Information and Archives directorate intranet site more along the lines of U.S. news librarians' intranets. But the difference is that this BBC computer-assisted research site will eventually serve not just news journalists here and in all the fifty or so foreign bureaus, but all BBC program makers in every genre, from dramas to soap operas, history programs, children's programs, science programs, and so forth. There are 23,000 staff in the BBC. The project pushes the library out much more onto the intranet, in terms of its value in validating Web sources. So, there's going to be a trusted Web guide that uses the criteria of currency, accuracy, and impartiality. Three computer-assisted searchers will be validating sources, and there are floor walkers, or coaches, too. Floor walkers are information professionals who go into programs, or any area of the BBC, and help people with the Internet or intranet at their desks.

It makes sense for the library people to work on that while you're in the thick of research for production.

Yes. They find it useful to use me as a consultant, because the library is often in a different building situated a long way away from where the program makers are. I'm much closer to the users. I'm part of the team and I understand how they think, the processes they go through, and the pressures they are under.

You really are the middleman, the one who knows what the journalists and reporters need.

Yes. The Internet has totally changed the way I am perceived on the program, and has totally changed my job. The chapter I wrote for the book, *Information Sources in the Press and Broadcast Media* [232], I called "From Gopher to Guru." Previously, I was considered a gopher, in that I ran up and down the roads to the library. The library was literally in a different building at that time, and I ran to the library to get photocopied press cuttings. So, I was somewhat hidden in the library; I was pushed into that clerical role and perceived as a service, whereas the Internet made information sexy, in a way. Suddenly, everyone values the skills that you have. Suddenly, they're interested in what you can do. So, I've become more visible. For a while, I was not perceived as really being one of the team, but now, they look up to me. I do a lot of desk training and encouraging them to do their own searching.

I'd like to talk a little bit about the relationships between journalists and librarians, because I think it's quite different in your country. The impression we get is that you work quite closely with the journalists. You call your news librarians "researchers," and researchers can have a library background; is that correct?

Yes. I find that it varies quite a bit. Some organizations are much further along in establishing collaborative environments. I'm also seeing many new titles for researchers, including research editor and research journalist.

I must say I like "information editor." I was an editor of information. There is a definite power struggle between journalists and librarians here, and I don't know if it's the same in the states. The power struggle is that we're both in the information-gathering business, but the way we approach information gathering is very different. Journalists like information straight from the horse's mouth. They like to get it from a primary source. A program like Panorama values what you would term "morgue" information—dead news, old news. Obviously we value that because that's what we're about, analysis and background. But most daily journalists just need it—I hesitate to say "quick and dirty," but they're interested in the primary source, right up to the minute, and getting to the story first. Deadline news is about feeding the beast, the news machine.

Librarians do more with secondary sources, books and cuttings and public sources. The way they go about gathering information is different, but ultimately the aim is the same. That's the reason for this conflict; we're both seekers and disseminators of information, but we go about it in different ways.

The dilemma of the investigative librarian is that I can't go to the most obvious source of information or I may alert someone. As a librarian, I'm naturally collaborative; I want to share my sources, help other librarians and information professionals. Journalists don't do that. Investigative journalists especially don't do that. They're very protective of their sources.

We've encountered this problem on the computer-assisted research project that I've been involved in. We're trying to encourage people to share their sources in a knowledge management context. You tell me about the Web site that you found really useful in putting this program together, and we'll give you an incentive to do that. The incentive that I came up with was to give them free credits for searching online Information and Archive databases that exist within the BBC.

In addition to filtering and validating Web sources, "Research Central" holds links to all the internal Information and Archives databases: NEON, the Internal BBC News cuttings database which Dialog runs; Elvis, the picture library database; MARS, the mood music database. You can search the BBC library book catalogue, you can search the BBC's own music library catalogue, and INFAX, the vast BBC Film and Videotape library and radio holdings database. All these databases are being pushed out to end users, so that they are doing more searching for themselves on our intranet. This obviously has an impact on the costing mechanisms between the BBC libraries and the users. It should be cheaper for the program makers to search for themselves.

We have a vast internal market system that was brought in under the previous Director General, John Birt, whereby everything has to be costed between departments. Every inquiry to the library, every spell check, every piece of research has to be quantified and charged back to that program, to that researcher, to that journalist. This is fine when you're charging it out to tangible things, like cameras and facilities and editing suites, but when you're actually trying to charge out intangible inquiries, it's quite difficult. How do you measure investigative research when a large percentage of it is not evident in the finished product—negative checks, dismissing lines of inquiry, and so on? The point is that there is a lot of financial pressure on journalists when they are using BBC services, including the library-run services, because everything is costed to their program budget. We now have a new BBC Director General, Greg

Dyke, and some of the internal market is being reduced—things are continually changing.

Another way to share more and save money that makes sense is that the Research Central computer-assisted research system on the intranet is brokering corporate-wide deals to commercial databases, trying to reduce the number of individual accounts all over the BBC. That is actually quite a challenge, because the BBC is so huge.

The big, big challenge is marketing the Research Central site, and training. Because the BBC is very large, and very disjointed, it's difficult trying to market the information. Floorwalkers, presentations, articles in the in-house magazine *Ariel* are just some of the ways.

If you were teaching a class of reporters right now, what are some of your best tips that you would share with them?

I would emphasize the point I made earlier about relying on the recognized news organizations. Go to them first and see what they have in terms of briefings, chronologies, and overviews. The BBC and CNN and Reuters—use them as your starting point because you know that they're traditional sources that are well-practiced in a news environment.

The SLA News Division's chart of all the newspaper library archives online [167] is a favorite resource for me, and one that I highly recommend. The big mistake that people make when they're searching for news on the Internet is not grasping the fact that newspapers have not put their archives going way back on the Internet for free—at least not yet—because they have lucrative deals with commercial databases. So, they waste a lot of time trying to find the article, or trying to find the news source and then trying to locate an archive. I always direct people to the SLA News Division newspaper archives site. Ideally though, if you are lucky enough to have it, use a commercial news database for news cuttings. Time is money.

Another recommendation I have is to use sources that have already been selected and validated for you as starting points, especially academic subject gateways. The ones we use are quite oriented to the U.K., such as PINAKES [144] and Resource Discovery Network [158]. They are compiled by U.K. academic librarians who are working together to catalogue subsets of the Internet. You find a high-quality subset of the Internet in subject areas such as social affairs, arts, and media. When you're searching for a social science story, you can search on the Social Science Information Gateway [168], and you know you're searching a quality subset of information.

Another tip is to learn to recognize how a URL is made up, with .gov, .edu, .org, and so forth. When you go through hits from a search engine, choose these first. Use government bodies, and political pressure groups as well, for story ideas. Pressure groups across the political spectrum have good Web sites, and their ideas and current research tend to drive policy, or at least feed into consultative documents that may drive policy. For example, on the left-wing side we have a group called Demos [43]. They are a really good source of story ideas, because their analysts and experts are identifying areas of future research. For example, parental leave is quite big in the news here right now. The key social affairs pressure groups will have looked at this in the last two years. I keep a bookmark list of all these pressure groups and check on them periodically. They're very good for long-term source stories. For current affairs, they also have press releases, so they can be quite useful in a deadline news environment as well.

Another point I would make to reporters is to never think that the Internet can replace printed sources. Use it in conjunction with them. Before you touch the keyboard and put in a broad term, *think*: Does this topic have an organization, trade body, help group, or relevant journal? Use a reference book to find the journal or the organization.

Lastly, know what type of information you are looking for, and only use a general search engine if you really want a very broad "brainstorming" approach. If you want a book, use something like Amazon [9]. If you just want news, use a news-only search engine, like News Index [137]. If you know you want a certain topic, learn the best portals for that type of information and use them as starting points. If you are looking for one specific Web site—that is, you know *exactly* what you want, the home page of a specific company or a specific government body—I would currently recommend using Google [80].

What advice would you give reporters and non-research people about using commercial database services?

Journalists want timely, accurate information pushed to them that they can use. They do not want to know all the information that is out there. Although many journalists do want to search for themselves, many do not have the time or inclination. They would rather delegate. The key is to know how much to do yourself, and when to delegate to an information professional. This will vary. We must continually work on the relationship between journalists and librarians, in that librarians have to gain trust from the journalists. This only happens when you work closely together. I had a particularly difficult relationship with one journalist who wouldn't trust that I knew the right source to look in. Also, he didn't want to tell me what he really wanted. We had the age-old problem of the inquiry interview, but also the absolute key problem that he didn't want to tell me what he really wanted, because he didn't want to give his story idea away to me. So, we have this sort of intermediary-end user wrestle about who actually wants to do the searching.

The Internet is breaking down some of these problems because of the move toward end-user searching with Web front ends. I think journalists feel much more empowered now and less resentful of having to delegate, because they're actually sitting at their own desks, searching Web front-end commercial databases, even though you're hovering around in the background, helping to steer them in the right direction. Two years ago, there'd be a separate dial-in terminal, and you'd be doing it and they'd be standing hovering behind you. That's a change.

How do you think research and reporting methods will change over the next few years?

Journalistically, one thing that worries me is the decline in time available for "real journalism"—in-depth reporting—as the pressure to feed the proliferation of outlets increases. I am talking in general here, not about the BBC necessarily. How many outlets can we stretch to—online, TV, radio, paper—rolling twenty-four-hour news? And will it be the money and time needed for in-depth analysis and investigation that will suffer as we continually strive to feed the appetite for live news in a twenty-four-hour society?

Another thing I am keeping my eye on is "open source journalism." I am trying not to close my mind to it. It derives from the idea of open source software, actually—anybody being able to "peer-review" and modify software that's out there on the Web. What's actually happening to some technology journalists is that they're writing stories, and the stories are being shaped by people on the Internet. Articles are posted, and viewpoints or angles within the article are changed according to feedback received by the author from the online community. I find this slightly worrisome. Does it remove the power of the editor? What is the future for quality journalism? Of course, it depends on the credentials of the community shaping the journalism. There are lots of quality control issues. I'm also quite skeptical about it, coming from an investigative journalism background; "open source" seems a contradiction in terms.

More positively for information professionals, I think research will move much more toward the end-user environment, with the librarians doing even more as facilitators and trainers. It's going to move much more toward the internal company intranets filtering the Internet for reporters. Though there's going to be more end-user searching, that doesn't mean there's going to be a decline in jobs for librarians. Quite the contrary; there's going to be even more of a demand for librarians as information editors and facilitators and specialists, who are going to become more visible.

Here in the U.K., researchers in news organizations, whether print or broadcasting, will continue to be almost exclusively journalists on the first rung of the ladder, and not information professionals, unless librarians shout from the rooftops about our Internet skills. We have a way into news research that didn't exist before. We can do this by working on program teams or as closely with journalists and program makers as we can. It should be a marriage of skills.

Super Searcher Power Tips

➤ I always tell people, even if you don't think you're an advanced searcher, use the advanced search capability, because it gives you more power and control over the way you search.

➤ The Net is exciting in terms of pictures, which can give you insight into a story. It can also provide ideas, tips, potential program contributors, and angles not found in the mainstream press.

➤ In order to stay on top of what sources are out there and what's new, I hardly ever search the Web. I rely on mailing lists.

➤ I advise relying on the recognized news organizations. Go to them first and see what they have in terms of briefings, chronologies, overviews. The BBC and CNN and Reuters—use them as the first starting point.

➤ A lot of time is wasted trying to find an article, or trying to find the news source and then trying to locate an archive. I always direct people to the SLA News Division newspaper archives site.

➤ Use sources that have already been selected and validated for you as starting points, especially academic subject gateways. You know you're searching a quality subset of information.

➤ Never think that the Internet can replace printed sources. Use it in conjunction with them. Use a reference book to find an organization, trade body, help group, or a relevant journal.

Appendix:
Referenced Sites and Sources

INTERNET SITES, SEARCH ENGINES, AND ONLINE DATABASES

1. **10-K Wizard**
    www.10kwizard.com

2. **192.com (U.K. directory)**
    www.192.com

3. **1stHeadlines**
    www.1stheadlines.com

4. **ABC News**
    www.abcnews.com

5. **Achoo!**
    www.achoo.com

6. **Alexa**
    www.alexa.com

7. **AltaVista**
    www.altavista.com

8. **AltaVista Advanced**
    www.altavista.com/cgi-bin/query?pg=aq

9. **Amazon.com**
    www.amazon.com

10. **America Online (AOL)**
    www.aol.com

11. **American Institute of Certified Public Accountants**
www.aicpa.org/

12. **American Medical Association**
www.ama-assn.org

13. **AnyWho (AT&T)**
www.anywho.com

14. **APBnews.com**
www.apbnews.com

15. **Art Museum.Net**
www.artmuseum.net

16. **Artnet.com**
www.artnet.com

17. **Ask Jeeves**
www.ask.com

18. **Associated Press**
www.ap.org

19. **Association of UK Media Librarians**
www.aukml.org

20. **AutoTrack**
www.autotrackxp.com

21. **Barbara Gellis Shapiro's News Researcher Site**
www.gate.net/~barbara/indext.htm

22. **BBC**
www.bbc.co.uk

23. **BBC Panorama**
www.bbc.co.uk/Panorama

24. **The BigHub**
www.thebighub.com

25. **Bloomberg**
www.bloomberg.com

26. **Bloomberg Business Video**
www.bloomberg.com/videos

27. **Bureau of National Affairs**
www.bna.com

28. **Business 2.0**
business2.com

29. **Cameo—U.K. Electoral Roll On-Line**
www.viaweb.com/p4l/ukelrolon.html

30. **CBS MarketWatch**
www.cbsmarketwatch.com

CDB Infotek
see ChoicePoint [31]

31. **ChoicePoint(formerly CDB Infotek)**
www.choicepointonline.com

32. **CIA World Factbook**
www.odci.gov/cia/publications/factbook/

33. **CNET**
www.cnet.com

34. **CNN—Cable News Network**
www.cnn.com

35. **CompuServe**
www.compuserve.com

36. **Cornell Law School Legal Information Institute** (U.S. Supreme Court Opinions)
supct.law.cornell.edu/supct/

37. **CyberClipping.com**
www.cyberclipping.com

38. **Cyber Paperboy**
www.cyberpaperboy.com

39. **The Daily Telegraph (U.K.)**
www.dailytelegraph.co.uk

40. **DataStar Web**
www.datastarweb.com

41. **DBT Online**
www.dbtonline.com

42. **Deja.com (formerly DejaNews)**
www.deja.com

43. **Demos**
www.demos.org

44. **DialogClassic**
www.dialogclassic.com

45. **DialogSelect**
     www.dialogselect.com

46. **Dialog Intranet Toolkit**
     products.dialog.com/products/toolkit/

47. **Dogpile**
     www.dogpile.com

48. **Dow Jones Interactive**
     djinteractive.com

49. **dowjones.com (now Work.com)**
     dowjones.wsj.com

50. **Dun & Bradstreet**
     www.dnb.com

51. **EBSCO*host***
     www.epnet.com

52. **EDGAR (Securities and Exchange Commission)**
     www.sec.gov/edgarhp.htm

53. **Encyclopaedia Britannica**
     www.britannica.com

54. **Encyclopedia of Associations**
     www.gale.com

55. **Environmental Working Group**
     www.ewg.org

56. **Evaluating Web Resources**
     by Jan Alexander and Marcia Ann Tate
     (Widener University, Wolfgram Memorial Library)
     www2.widener.edu/Wolfgram-Memorial-Library/webeval.htm

57. **Evaluating Web Resources – Checklist for a News Web Page**
     www2.widener.edu/Wolfgram-Memorial-Library/news.htm

58. **Excite**
     excite.com

59. **Excite NewsTracker**
     nt.excite.com

60. **ExpertNet**
     www.cvcp.ac.uk/WhatWeDo/ExpertNet/expertnet.html

61. **Facts on File**
     www.facts.com

62. **Fast Company**
www.fastcompany.com

63. **FAST Search**
www.fast.no or www.alltheweb.com

64. **FedStats**
www.fedstats.gov

65. **FedWorld**
www.fedworld.gov

66. **Financial Times**
www.ft.com

67. **FindLaw**
www.findlaw.com

68. **Florida Department of Corrections**
www.dc.state.fl.us

69. **Forrester Research**
www.forrester.com

70. **Fox News**
www.foxnews.com/video

71. **FreeEDGAR**
www.freeedgar.com

72. **Free Pint**
www.freepint.co.uk

73. **FT Profile (now part of Lexis-Nexis Europe)**
www.info.ft.com

74. **Gale Biography Resource Center**
www.gale.com

75. **GaleNet**
galenet.gale.com/

76. **Gary Price's Direct Search**
gwis2.circ.gwu.edu/~gprice/direct.htm

77. **Gary Price's List of Lists**
gwis2.circ.gwu.edu/~gprice/listof.htm

78. **Global NewsBank**
www.newsbank.com

79. **Go.com**
www.go.com

80. **Google**
www.google.com

81. **Google—Uncle Sam**
www.google.com/unclesam

82. **GovSearch (Northern Light)**
usgovsearch.northernlight.com/publibaccess/

83. **Handspring**
www.handspring.com

84. **HMSO (Her Majesty's Stationery Office)**
www.hmso.gov.uk

85. **Hoover's Online**
www.hoovers.com

86. **HotBot**
www.hotbot.com

87. **Humanities Index**
www.hwwilson.com

88. **Human Rights Watch**
www.hrw.org

89. **IDG.net**
www.idg.net

90. **The Industry Standard**
www.thestandard.com

91. **InferenceFind**
www.inferencefind.com

92. **Informant**
informant.dartmouth.edu

93. **Information Today Inc. NewsBreaks**
www.infotoday.com/newsbreaks

94. **InfoSpace**
www.infospace.com

95. **InfoUSA**
www.infousa.com

96. **Institute for War and Peace Reporting**
www.iwpr.net/index.pl5?home_index.html

97. **The Internet Newsroom**
www.editors-service.com

98. **Investext**
www.investext.com

99. **Investigative Reporters and Editors (IRE)**
www.ire.org

100. **Ireland, Government of—Good Friday Agreement**
www.irlgov.ie/iveagh/angloirish/goodfriday/default.htm

IRS—Form 990
see National Center for Charitable Statistics [128]

101. **Jupiter Communications**
www.jup.com

102. **Keesing's Online Database**
www.keesings.com

103. **Knight Ridder**
www.kri.com

104. **KRT Business News**
www.krtdirect.com

105. **LawCrawler**
www.lawcrawler.com

106. **Lexis-Nexis**
www.lexis-nexis.com

107. **Lexis-Nexis Universe**
web.lexis-nexis.com/ln.universe

108. **Librarian's Index to the Internet—Keeping up with New Internet Resources**
lii.org/search/file/newsites

109. **Librarian's Index to the Internet—New this Week**
lii.org

110. **The London Times**
www.thetimes.co.uk

111. **Liszt**
www.liszt.com

112. **The Louvre**
www.louvre.fr

113. **Lycos**
www.lycos.com

114. **Mailbase**
    www.mailbase.ac.uk

115. **Mamma**
    www.mamma.com

116. **MapBlast**
    www.mapblast.com

117. **MapQuest**
    www.mapquest.com

118. **Martindale-Hubbell Lawyer Locator**
    www.martindale.com

119. **MEDLINE**
    www.nlm.nih.gov/medlineplus/

120. **MetaCrawler**
    www.metacrawler.com

121. **MetaFind**
    www.metafind.com

122. **Metropolitan Museum (NY)**
    www.metmuseum.org

123. **The Miami Herald**
    www.herald.com

124. **The Miami Herald (archive on NewsLibrary)**
    www.herald.com/newslibrary/

125. **MSNBC**
    www.msnbc.com

126. **Multex.com**
    www.multex.com

127. **My Simon**
    www.mysimon.com

128. **National Center for Charitable Statistics (IRS—Form 990)**
    www.urban.org/990

129. **National Institute for Computer-Assisted Reporting (NICAR)**
    www.nicar.org

130. **National Public Radio (NPR)**
    www.npr.org

131. **NATO**
    www.nato.org

132. **Needle in a CyberStack**
     members.home.net/albeej/

133. **New York Times Online**
     www.nytimes.com

134. **NewsBank NewsFile**
     www.newsbank.com

135. **NewsBot**
     www.newsbot.com

136. **NewsHub**
     www.newshub.com

137. **News Index**
     www.newsindex.com

138. **NewsTrawler**
     www.newstrawler.com

139. **Nobel Prize**
     www.nobel.se/prize/

140. **Northern Light**
     www.nlsearch.com

141. **NRA (National Rifle Association)**
     www.nra.org

142. **PCMike.com**
     www.pcmike.com

143. **Penal Lexicon**
     www.penlex.org.uk

144. **PINAKES, a Subject Launchpad**
     www.hw.ac.uk/libWWW/irn/pinakes/pinakes.html

145. **Power Reporting Alerts by Email**
     PowerReporting.com/category/Alerts_by_E-mail

146. **Poynter Institute for Media Studies**
     www.poynter.org

147. **PR Newswire**
     www.prnewswire.com

148. **ProfNet**
     www.profnet.com

149. **ProFusion**
     www.profusion.com

150. **Project Gutenberg**
www.gutenberg.net

151. **ProQuest**
www.proquest.com/proquest

152. **Public Records Online, A ChoicePoint Company**
www.flpro.com

153. **Radio and Television News Directors Association**
www.rtnda.org

154. **Real Cities Network**
www.realcities.com

155. **Red Herring**
www.redherring.com

156. **RemarQ**
www.remarq.com

157. **Reporter's Desktop**
www.reporter.org/desktop

158. **Resource Discovery Network**
www.rdn.ac.uk

159. **Reuters**
www.reuters.com

160. **The Right-to-Know Network**
www.rtk.net

161. **San Jose Mercury News**
www.mercurycenter.com
(News Hound is no longer available. Sign up for E-Mail Dispatches from the home page shown above.)

162. **Seattle Times, Special Project series by Duff Wilson, "Fear in the Fields"**
www.seattletimes.com/news/special/#fields

163. **SiliconValley.com**
www.mercurycenter.com/svtech/

164. **SIRS (Social Issues Resources Series)**
www.sirs.com

165. **SLA News Division**
metalab.unc.edu/slanews

166. **SLA News Division—Newspapers Online**
metalab.unc.edu/slanews/internet/papersal.html

167. **SLA News Division—U.S. News Archives on the Web**
metalab.unc.edu/slanews/internet/archives.html

168. **SOSIG—Social Science Information Gateway**
www.sosig.ac.uk

169. **Stanford Securities Class Action Clearinghouse**
(Robert Crown Law Library, Stanford University School of Law)
securities.stanford.edu

170. **Sun-Sentinel**
www.sun-sentinel.com

171. **Switchboard**
www.switchboard.com

172. **Tate Gallery**
www.tate.org.uk

173. **TheStreet.com**
www.thestreet.com

174. **Thomas (U.S. Library of Congress)**
thomas.loc.gov/

175. **Time, Inc.**
www.time-inc.com

176. **Tony Awards**
www.tonys.org

177. **TotalNEWS**
www.totalnews.com

178. **UCLA College Library Instruction**
Thinking Critically about World Wide Web Resources, by Esther
Grassian
www.library.ucla.edu/libraries/college/instruct/web/critical.htm

179. **U.K. Central Office of Information**
www.coi.gov.uk

180. **U.K. Ministry of Defence**
www.mod.uk

181. **U.K. Online User Group**
www.ukolug.org.uk

182. **U.K. Plus**
www.ukplus.co.uk

183. **Ultimate Pro-Life Resource List**
www.prolifeinfo.org

184. **Uniform Crime Reports (FBI)**
www.fbi.gov/ucr.htm

185. **U.S. Department of Agriculture**
www.usda.gov

186. **U.S. Department of Commerce**
www.doc.gov

187. **U.S. Equal Employment Opportunity Commission**
www.eeoc.gov

188. **U.S. Federal Aviation Administration**
FAA Civil Aviation Registry
registry.faa.gov

189. **U.S. Federal Election Commission**
www.fec.gov

190. **U.S. Food and Drug Administration**
www.usda.gov

191. **U.S. Government Printing Office**
www.gpo.gov

192. **U.S. National Oceanic and Atmospheric Administration (NOAA)**
www.noaa.gov

193. **U.S. National Weather Service**
www.nws.noaa.gov

194. **U.S. Securities and Exchange Commission**
sec.gov

195. **U.S. State Department**
www.state.gov

196. **U.S. Supreme Court**
www.supremecourtus.gov

197. **Wall Street Journal Interactive**
wsj.com

198. **Washington Document Service**
wdsdocs.com

199. **The Washington Post**
www.washingtonpost.com

200. **The Weather Channel**
www.weather.com

201. **Webfeat**
www.webfeat.com

202. **Westlaw**
www.westlaw.com

203. **Whois (from Network Solutions)**
www.networksolutions.com/cgi-bin/whois/whois

204. **Wilson Biographies**
www.hwwilson.com

205. **Wired**
www.wired.com

206. **Yahoo!**
www.yahoo.com

207. **Yahoo! Alerts**
alerts.yahoo.com

208. **Yahoo! GeoCities**
geocities.yahoo.com

209. **Yahoo! News**
dailynews.yahoo.com

210. **Yahoo! What's New**
www.yahoo.com/new/

211. **ZDNet**
www.zdnet.com

ELECTRONIC DISCUSSION GROUPS, MAILING LISTS AND NEWSLETTERS

212. **CARR-L (Computer Assisted Research and Reporting)**
To subscribe, send email to
LISTSERV@ULKYVM.LOUISVILLE.EDU
In message body type:
SUBscribe CARR-L Your-real-name Organization

213. **China News Digest**
www.cnd.org

214. **IDG.net**
www.idg.net

215. **The Internet TOURBUS**
www.tourbus.com

216. **IRE-L** (Investigative Reporters and Editors)
To subscribe, send email to
listproc@lists.missouri.edu
In message body type:
SUB IRE-L Firstname Lastname

217. **Net-happenings** (Gleason Sackmann)
listserv.classroom.com/archives/net-happenings.html (archive)
scout.cs.wisc.edu/caservices/net-hap/index.html

218. **NICAR-L** (National Institute for Computer-Assisted Reporting)
To subscribe, send email to
listproc@lists.missouri.edu
In message body type:
SUB NICAR-L Firstname Lastname

219. **ResearchBuzz (From Tara Calishain)**
www.researchbuzz.com/news/index.html

220. **The Scout Report**
scout.cs.wisc.edu/index.html
scout.cs.wisc.edu/misc/subscribe.html

221. **Search Engine Watch (Danny Sullivan)**
www.searchenginewatch.com

222. **SLA News Division**
To subscribe, send email to
listproc@listserv.oit.unc.edu
In message body type:
subscribe NEWSLIB firstname lastname

223. **The Sports Business Daily**
www.sportsbizdaily.com

224. **Stumpers-L**
To subscribe, send email to:
mailserv@cuis.edu
In message body type:
subscribe STUMPERS-L YourEmailAddress

225. **Wired News Daily**
To subscribe, visit hotwired.lycos.com

OTHER RESOURCES

226. *Computer Assisted Research: A Guide to Tapping Online Information (4th Edition)*

By Nora M. Paul
Bonus Books Inc. and Poynter Institute, St. Petersburg, FL, 1999
www.poynter.org/pub/car.htm

227. *EContent* (formerly *Database*)
Online Inc., Wilton, CT, bimonthly
www.ecmag.net
www.onlineinc.com/database (archives)

228. *Encyclopedia of Associations*
Gale Research, Farmington Hills, MI, 2000
www.gale.com

229. *Facts on File Weekly World News Digest*
Facts on File News Service, New York, NY, weekly
www.factsonfile.com

230. *Fulltext Sources Online*
Information Today, Inc., Medford, NJ, 2x year
www.infotoday.com/catalog/direct.htm

231. *Great Scouts! CyberGuides for Subject Searching on the Web*
By Nora Paul & Margot Williams
Information Today, Inc., Medford, NJ, 1999
www.infotoday.com/catalog/books.htm

232. *Information Sources for the Press and Broadcast Media*
Edited by Sarah Adair
Bowker-Saur, 1999
http://www.bowker-saur.co.uk/

233. *Information Today*
Information Today, Inc., Medford, NJ, monthly
www.infotoday.com/it

234. *Internet World*
Penton Media, Westport, CT, weekly
www.iw.com

235. *Online*
Online Inc., Wilton, CT, bimonthly
www.onlineinc.com/onlinemag

236. *PC World*
www.pcworld.com

237. *Searcher*
Information Today, Inc., Medford, NJ, 10x/year.
www.infotoday.com/searcher

238. ***Secrets of the Super Searchers***
By Reva Basch
CyberAge Books, Information Today Inc., Medford, NJ, 1993
www.infotoday.com/catalog/books.htm

239. ***Secrets of the Super Net Searchers***
By Reva Basch
CyberAge Books, Information Today Inc., Medford, NJ, 1996
www.infotoday.com/catalog/books.htm

240. ***Who's Who in America***
Marquis Who's Who, New Providence, NJ, annual
www.marquiswhoswho.com

241. ***The Wired Journalist: Newsroom Guide to the Internet*** (revised third edition)
By Mike Wendland
www.rtndf.org/rtndf/wiredweb

242. ***The World Almanac and Book of Facts***
Edited by Robert Famighetti
www.worldalmanac.com

243. ***Yahoo! Internet Life***
ZDNet, monthly
www.zdnet.com/yil/

SOFTWARE

244. **Associated Press Broadcast Technology (ENPS)**
www.enps.com

245. **Autonomy**
www.autonomy.com

246. **Cold Fusion (Allaire Corp.)**
www.allaire.com/Products/index.cfm

247. **Copernic**
www.copernic.com

248. **Enfish Tracker Pro**
www.enfish.com

249. **Homesite (Allaire Corp.)**
www.allaire.com/Products/index.cfm

250. **Intelliseek BullsEye**
www.intelliseek.com

251. **Internet FastFind** (Symantec Corp.)
     www.symantec.com

252. **Microsoft Access**
     www.microsoft.com/office/access/

253. **Microsoft Excel**
     www.microsoft.com/office/excel/

254. **SII** (System Integrators, Inc.)
     www.sii.com

255. **WebRecord Research Pro** (Canon Computer Systems, Inc.)
     www.software.canon.com

About the Author

As Contributing Editor of *Information Today*—the leading monthly publication covering the online information industry—Paula Hane writes news features, conducts interviews, edits a section of the paper on Internet publishing, and writes breaking news stories for the Information Today Web site. For eight years, she was the Editor of *DATABASE* magazine, and served on the planning board of the annual Online World Conference & Exposition. As a working reporter covering the online information industry, software, databases, technology, and libraries, she understands both the tools/techniques of the modern news researcher and the demanding day-to-day pressures of the profession. Paula has an M.L.S. from Columbia University and a Masters in English from NYU. She lives in Plano, Texas.

About the Editor

Reva Basch, executive editor of the Super Searchers series, is a writer, researcher, and consultant to the online industry. She is the author of the original Super Searcher books, *Secrets of the Super Searchers* and *Secrets of the Super Net Searchers*, as well as *Researching Online For Dummies* and *Electronic Information Delivery: Ensuring Quality and Value*. She writes the "Reva's (W)rap" column for *ONLINE* magazine, has contributed numerous articles and columns to professional journals and the popular press, and has keynoted at conferences in Europe, Scandinavia, Australia, Canada, and the U.S.

A past president of the Association of Independent Information Professionals, she has a Master's in Library Science from the University of California at Berkeley and more than 20 years of experience in database and Internet research. Basch was Vice President and Director of Research at Information on Demand and has been president of her own company, Aubergine Information Services, since 1986.

Index

W

The Wall Street Journal
  access to, 90, 154
  accuracy and integrity, 38–39
  business spiders, 29
  on Dow Jones Interactive, 71
  Story, 162
  Web site, 43
  wireless connections, 143
Wall Street Journal Interactive, 43
Washington Document Service (WDS), 72
The Washington Post, 79, 98–100,
    107–108, 185–186
Washington Post-Newsweek Television,
    131, 132
The Washington Quarterly, 160
WashingtonPost.com, 92
Watergate clipping files, 109
WDIV-TV, 131
Weather Channel, 24
Web sites. *see also* Internet
  beat approach, 41
  crashes, 125
  identification of creators, 199
  updates, 159
Webcasts, 132
Webfeat.com, 164
WebRecord Research Pro, 58
Wendland, Michael, 131–146
  access to information, 140–141
  background, 131–133
  bookmarks management, 133
  effect of the technology, 10
  electronic mailing lists, 134
  on interactivity, 141–142
  intranet authority and integrity, 135
  obtaining government information,
    137–139
  power tips, 145–146
  at the Poyner Institute, 5
  research examples, 136–137
  research strategies, 133–135
  research trends, 139–140, 142–144
  staying current, 139
Westlaw, 34
Wetware, 25
Whois, 92, 135
Who's Who, 92, 160, 164
Widener, 159

Williams, Margot
  acknowledgment, xv
  articles for *Database,* 1
  background, 85–87
  credit for research, 97
  favorite project, 97–98
  Great Scouts!, 2, 28, 92
  international training by, 5, 85–106
  intranet management, 98–100
  new developments on the Internet,
    93–95
  power tips, 105–106
  Pulitzer Prize, 8
  research strategies, 87–92
  searching by journalists and
    researchers, 95–97
  staying updated, 101–102
  trends, 103–105
  verification of sources, 92–93
Wilson, Duff, 51–65
  alert services, 57–58
  background, 51–52
  favorite projects, 61–63
  information searching, 52–53
  integrity and authority of sources, 60
  Internet frustrations, 63–64
  intranet management, 54–56
  keeping up-to-date, 58–59
  new developments on the Internet, 61
  news urgency in the Internet, 63
  power tips, 65
  Reporter's Desktop site, 5, 53–54, 59
  resource choice, 57–58
  search strategies, 57–58
  Seattle Times, The, 51–52
  teamwork model, 56
  trends in researching and reporting, 64
  use of commercial services, 52
  working with librarians, 54
Wilson Biographies Online, 176
Wired, 42, 134
The Wired Journalist (Wendland), 133
Wired News, 143
Wireless connecting, 133
Wolfgram Memorial Library, 18
Woodward, Bob, 109
Workers compensation records, 111
World Almanac, 24

More CyberAge Books
from Information Today, Inc.

Great Scouts!
CyberGuides for Subject Searching on the Web

Nora Paul and Margot Williams • Edited by Paula J. Hane

Great Scouts! is a cure for information overload. Authors Nora Paul (The Poynter Institute) and Margot Williams *(The Washington Post)* direct readers to the very best subject-specific, Web-based information resources. Thirty chapters cover specialized "CyberGuides" selected as the premier Internet sources of information on business, education, arts and entertainment, science and technology, health and medicine, politics and government, law, sports, and much more. With its expert advice and evaluations of information and link content, value, currency, stability, and usability, *Great Scouts!* takes you "beyond search engines"—and directly to the top sources of information for your topic. As a reader bonus, the authors are maintaining a Web page featuring updated links to all the sites covered in the book.

Softbound • ISBN 0-910965-27-7 • $24.95

Electronic Democracy
Using the Internet to Influence American Politics

Graeme Browning

Here is everything you need to know to become a powerful player in the political process from your desktop. Experienced Washington reporter Graeme Browning (National Journal, Center for Democracy & Technology) offers real-world strategies for using the World Wide Web to reach and influence decision makers inside the Beltway. Loaded with practical tips, techniques, and case studies, this is a must-read for anyone interested in the future of representative government and the marriage of technology and politics.

Softbound • ISBN 0-910965-20-X • $19.95

Super Searchers on Health & Medicine
The Online Secrets of Top Health & Medical Researchers

Susan M. Detwiler • Edited by Reva Basch

With human lives depending on them, skilled medical researchers rank among the best online searchers in the world. In *Super Searchers on Health & Medicine,* medical librarians, clinical researchers, health information specialists, and physicians explain how they combine traditional sources with the best of the Net to deliver just what the doctor ordered. If you use the Internet and online databases to answer important health and medical questions, these Super Searchers will help guide you around the perils and pitfalls to the best sites, sources, and techniques. As a reader bonus, "The Super Searchers Web Page" provides links to the most important Internet resources for health & medical researchers.

Softbound • ISBN 0-910965-44-7 • $24.95

Super Searchers on Wall Street
Top Investment Professionals Share Their Online Research Secrets

Amelia Kassel • Edited by Reva Basch

Through her probing interviews, Amelia Kassel reveals the online secrets of ten leading financial industry research experts. You'll learn how information professionals find and analyze market and industry data, as well as how online information is used by brokerages, stock exchanges, investment banks, and individual investors to make critical investment decisions. The Wall Street Super Searchers direct you to important sites and sources, illuminate the trends that are revolutionizing financial research, and help you use online research as part of a powerful investment strategy. As a reader bonus, a directory of top sites and sources is hyperlinked and periodically updated on the Web.

Softbound • ISBN 0-910965-42-0 • $24.95

Law of the Super Searchers
The Online Secrets of Top Legal Researchers

T.R. Halvorson • Edited by Reva Basch

In their own words, eight of the world's leading legal researchers explain how they use the Internet and online services to approach, analyze, and carry through a legal research project. In interviewing the experts, practicing attorney and online searcher T.R. Halvorson avoids the typical introductory approach to online research and focuses on topics critical to lawyers and legal research professionals: documenting the search, organizing a strategy, what to consider before logging on, efficient ways to build a search, and much more. *Law of the Super Searchers* offers fundamental strategies for legal researchers who need to take advantage of the wealth of information available online.

Softbound • ISBN 0-910965-34-X • $24.95

Super Searchers Do Business
The Online Secrets of Top Business Researchers

Mary Ellen Bates • Edited by Reva Basch

Super Searchers Do Business probes the minds of 11 leading researchers who use the Internet and online services to find critical business information. Through her in-depth interviews, Mary Ellen Bates—a business super searcher herself—gets the pros to reveal how they choose online sources, evaluate search results, and tackle the most challenging business research projects. Loaded with expert tips, techniques, and strategies, this is the first title in the exciting new "Super Searchers" series, edited by Reva Basch. If you do business research online, or plan to, let the Super Searchers be your guides.

Softbound• ISBN 0-910965-33-1 • $24.95

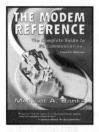

The Modem Reference, 4th Edition
The Complete Guide to PC Communications

Michael A. Banks

"If you can't find the answer to a telecommunications problem here, there probably isn't an answer."
—Lawrence Blasko, The Associated Press

Now in its 4th edition, this popular handbook explains the concepts behind computer data, data encoding, and transmission; providing practical advice for PC users who want to get the most from their online operations. In his uniquely readable style, author and techno-guru Mike Banks *(The Internet Unplugged)* takes readers on a tour of PC data communications technology, explaining how modems, fax machines, computer networks, and the Internet work. He provides an in-depth look at how data are communicated between computers all around the world, demystifying the terminology, hardware, and software. *The Modem Reference* is a must-read for students, professional online users, and all computer users who want to maximize their PC fax and data communications capability.

Softbound • ISBN 0-910965-36-6 • $29.95

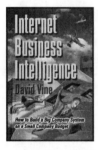

Internet Business Intelligence
How to Build a Big Company System on a Small Company Budget

David Vine

According to author David Vine, business success in the competitive, global marketplace of the 21st century will depend on a firm's ability to use information effectively—and the most successful firms will be those that harness the Internet to create and maintain a powerful information edge. In Internet Business Intelligence, Vine explains how any company—large or small—can build a complete, low-cost Internet-based business intelligence system that really works. If you're fed up with Internet hype and wondering "where's the beef?," you'll appreciate this savvy, no-nonsense approach to using the Internet to solve everyday business problems and to stay one step ahead of the competition.

Softbound • ISBN 0-910965-35-8 • $29.95

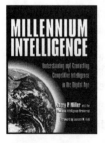

Millennium Intelligence
Understanding & Conducting Competitive Intelligence in the Digital Age

Jerry P. Miller and the Business Intelligence Braintrust

With contributions from the world's leading business intelligence practitioners, here is a tremendously informative and practical look at the CI process, how it is changing, and how it can be managed effectively in the Digital Age. Loaded with case studies, tips, and techniques, chapters include What Is Intelligence?; The Skills Needed to Execute Intelligence Effectively; Information Sources Used for Intelligence; The Legal and Ethical Aspects of Intelligence; Small Business Intelligence; Corporate Security and Intelligence; ... and much more!

Softbound • ISBN 0-910965-28-5 • $29.95

Internet Blue Pages, 2001-2002 Edition
The Guide to Federal Government Web Sites

Laurie Andriot

With over 1,800 Web addresses, this guide is designed to help you find any agency easily. Arranged in accordance with the US Government Manual, each entry includes the name of the agency, the Web address (URL), a brief description of the agency, and links to the agency's or subagency's home page. For helpful cross-referencing, an alphabetical agency listing and a comprehensive index for subject searching are also included. Regularly updated information and links are provided on the author's Web site.

Softbound • ISBN 0-910965-29-3 • $34.95

net.people
The Personalities and Passions Behind the Web Sites

Thomas E. Bleier and Eric C. Steinert

With the explosive growth of the Internet, people from all walks of life are bringing their dreams and schemes to life as Web sites. In *net.people*, authors Bleier and Steinert take you up close and personal with the creators of 35 of the world's most intriguing online ventures. For the first time, these entrepreneurs and visionaries share their personal stories and hard-won secrets of Webmastering. You'll learn how each of them launched a home page, increased site traffic, geared up for e-commerce, found financing, dealt with failure and success, built new relationships—and discovered that a Web site had changed their life forever.

Softbound • ISBN 0-910965-37-4 • $19.95

The Extreme Searcher's Guide To
Web Search Engines
A Handbook for the Serious Searcher

Randolph Hock

"Extreme searcher" Randolph (Ran) Hock—internationally respected Internet trainer and authority on Web search engines—offers advice designed to help you get immediate results. Ran not only shows you what's "under the hood" of the major search engines, but explains their relative strengths and weaknesses, reveals their many (and often overlooked) special features, and offers tips and techniques for searching the Web more efficiently and effectively than ever. Updates and links are provided at the author's Web site.

Softbound • ISBN 0-910965-26-9 • $24.95   Hardcover • ISBN 0-910965-38-2 • $34.95